Johnny Cornflakes

A Story about Loving the Unloved

An absolutely wonderful story and beautifully told.

The deep things in this simple story tug hard at the heart.

A tale of pathos and need, of joy and pain, of poverty and glorious abundance.

Johnny Cornflakes

A Story about Loving the Unloved

DENISE GEORGE

CHRISTIAN
FOCUS

A prolific and inspirational writer, Denise George is well known for writing books that are creative and biblical. Her husband Timothy is the executive editor of *Christianity Today* and is the founding dean of Beeson Divinity school. They live in Birmingham, Alabama.

Copyright © Denise George

ISBN 1-84550-551-4
ISBN 978-1-84550-551-6

10 9 8 7 6 5 4 3 2 1

Published in 2010
by
Christian Focus Publications,
Geanies House, Fearn,
Ross-shire, IV20 1TW Scotland

www.christianfocus.com

Cover design by Moose77.com

Printed by
Bell and Bain, Glasgow

Mixed Sources
Product group from well-managed forests and other controlled sources
www.fsc.org Cert no.TT-COC-002769
© 1996 Forest Stewardship Council

CONTENTS

"I tell you the truth, whatever you did for one of the least of these brothers of mine, you did for me." (Jesus, Matt. 25:40)

In the center of our family room bookcase rests an old, dirty shoe. It has a large gaping hole in the toe and a sheet of cardboard stuffed in the sole. The shoe—dirty and worn—has been a treasure of mine for more than 35 years. It reminds me of a time when I was young, arrogant, and unlovable, yet I was deeply loved by a most unusual person. And his unexpected and unconditional love pried open my prejudice-blinded eyes and forever changed my heart.

Introduction

Dear reader:

I grew up in a traditional family, with strong Christian values, in a beautiful Chattanooga, Tennessee, suburb. As a child and young woman, my parents purposely sheltered me, and somehow protected me from all of life's inevitable hardships. I spent my first 19 years living in a "kind world", surrounded by loving parents, caring maternal grandparents, aunts, uncles, cousins, and lots of close family friends. I always felt safe, secure, and deeply loved.

The segregated Southern United States, before the 1964 Civil Rights Act, kept the races separated. From kindergarten to 12th grade, my classmates had faces that looked like mine—lily white—and lifestyles that resembled mine—safe suburbs with two cars parked in the garage. In 1964, city officials finally removed the "Coloreds only" and "Whites only" signs from public toilets, water fountains, bus stations, and other public facilities. The offensive, divisive signs came down, but it took decades for hearts to change and true integration to happen in my city. I traveled mostly by car during those early years. I had never ridden a city bus.

In 1970, at my church, the Flintstone Baptist Church, I met Timothy, a college sophomore at the University of Tennessee at Chattanooga. We dated, fell in love, and married a year later. After his 1972 college graduation, we moved to Chelsea, a crime-laded, dirty inner city on the outskirts of Boston, Massachusetts. Harvard Divinity School had accepted him to begin work on a three-year Master of Divinity degree. I agreed to go in spite of my apprehensions and my secret fears of moving to an unknown city so far from home.

Twelve hundred miles away, my safe, secure world turned upside down. I no longer felt protected. I saw few white faces. Our inner city neighbors had skin of many colors and customs from world-wide places. They spoke languages I couldn't even identify. Impoverished families – children, teens, unwed mothers – meet me everywhere I turned. I saw suffering, violence, and hunger first-hand on the filthy streets of Chelsea. For the first few months there, I refused to unpack my dishes. I stayed in a state of shock.

Timothy took a position with the Home Mission Board of the Southern Baptist Convention so we could afford groceries. It paid little, but provided a large empty church building for worship services, and a small one-family parsonage for us to live in. Timothy became pastor of that church, the First Baptist Church of Chelsea. In our first Sunday church worship service we had eight people attend. And that number included Timothy and me! Mere survival, not God, proved more important to people in Chelsea.

I took a secretarial job at the Children's Community Corner child care center that met in the basement of the grand old First Baptist Church of Chelsea. I worked hard, and I cried much over the children's desperate needs and fragmented family lives.

Throughout my years in Chelsea, God began to teach me to "see" others with His eyes. Directly in my daily path God placed a mysterious, smelly, and pestering old man—Johnny Cornflakes. The town drunk, Johnny, bummed his way from house to house, trash bin to city trash bin, in search of cereal crumbs and daily sustenance. As far as I knew at that time, Johnny had no home, no possessions. At night he slept in cardboard boxes or in back alleys behind Chelsea's restaurants. Johnny proved one ugly, unlovable creature. And, for a while, the nasty sight of him brought vomit to my throat.

Before Timothy and I left Chelsea, Massachusetts however, Johnny Cornflakes would teach me a lesson in loving the unloved that I could never have learned in the safe, clean, segregated suburbs of Chattanooga, Tennessee. Through Johnny Cornflakes, God changed my heart. Forever. I have many times since thanked God for my "Chelsea experience" for our desperate hardships, empty stomachs, and rich teachable moments.

From Chelsea, we moved to Louisville, Kentucky, where Timothy taught church history at Southern Baptist Theological Seminary. I gave birth to two children at Louisville's Baptist Hospital East during those nine years there.

Throughout those years, I kept Johnny's memory very close to my heart. I wondered where he was, if he were still alive. I found my answer on the Sunday we traveled back to visit Chelsea and the First Baptist Church.

From Louisville, we moved to Birmingham, Alabama. Timothy founded a divinity school, Beeson Divinity School, on the campus of Samford University. I enrolled my young children in kindergarten and first grade, and spent most of my time taking care of my family. I stayed busy cooking, cleaning, carpooling children, going to church, teaching Sunday School, etc. But, for some reason, Johnny Cornflakes always stayed on my heart and mind while I raced around doing the work wives and moms do.

On the day before Thanksgiving, 1995, my activities stopped. Doctors at Brookwood Hospital performed successful major surgery on me. But due to some surgical complications, the recovery time proved very long—almost eight months. While I lay flat on my back, my incisions and internal organs healing, I had plenty of time to think. I thought again about my experiences with Johnny Cornflakes so many years ago.

"Tell Johnny's story, Denise," God seemed to be saying to my heart. "Write it down so that the whole world will learn what Johnny Cornflakes taught you about genuinely loving others—especially unloved others."

Day after day, God-directed thoughts about Johnny flooded my mind. I finally pulled my computer into my bed, and in spite of physical discomfort and pain, I started to write. I wrote for weeks from my bed until I finished the story of Johnny Cornflakes.

But nothing happened. My body healed and my active life resumed. Five years passed. God sent no interested publishers my way. I wondered if I had really received God's direction to write it. The manuscript lay on my desk gathering dust. Then, no doubt due to God's intervention, my friend Dr. Dellanna O'Brien, executive director of the Woman's Missionary Union, offered to read the manuscript. She liked it, and took it to WMU's New Hope Publishers.

They published the little volume, and kept it in print for several years. By the time the book had gone out of print, a small United States audience had bought and read it.

Now, in 2010, to my great delight, Christian Focus Publications has decided to republish the story – for the whole world to read. I guess God isn't finished with Johnny's story. I pray that the book will touch many more lives with God's simple and incredible message of love.

I wrote *Johnny Cornflakes: A Story about Loving the Unloved* for individuals to read, but also for families to read together. The story's message provides many teachable moments for parents and grandparents to talk about God and life and love with their children and grandchildren. It's a simple story, but one that tugs at the heart and may even change a life. I hope so.

My deep appreciation goes to all those people who made the book possible: my family, my friends, my publishers, and a bevy of readers who loved the story and shared it with others. And my special gratitude goes to God alone, who encouraged my heart to simply "tell Johnny's story".

Denise George
Birmingham, Alabama
January 1, 2010

(Note: The book is based on fact. However, some of the names have been changed to protect privacy, and some of the time sequences and events have been rearranged, shortened, or lengthened for clearer communication and more interesting reading.)

Chapter 1

The Long Journey North

Johnny Cornflakes wasn't his real name. No one knew his real name, or where he came from, or where he went each evening when the sun went down. The inner city street kids had long ago dubbed the tired old man "Johnny Cornflakes" and the name stuck. Johnny lived on the streets and daily searched for bits of thrown-away food in the city's trash bins. He especially liked the few remaining flakes in discarded cereal boxes—thus earning him the surname "Cornflakes".

Sometimes Grady, the owner of Grady's "Greasy Spoon" Diner down the street, tossed Johnny some crusty tidbits left on customers' plates. They proved delicacies to Johnny—five stars better than his usual scraps. I didn't care much for Grady. He was a mean old man, used four-lettered language, and kept an unfiltered cigarette dangling from his lips. An array of tattoos – ugly and indecent – covered both his arms. They confessed a wordless history of his tough life. So that everyone could see the cheap blue ink-art, he wore armpit-yellowed sleeveless t-shirts. But Grady was good to Johnny Cornflakes, and Johnny loved the foul old cook and bottle-washer.

My husband, Timothy, and I, native Southerners, had traveled to New England to work and study. Timothy had been accepted at the prestigious Harvard Divinity School in Cambridge, Massachusetts, to work on a Master of Divinity degree. Those were the days, back in the early 1970s, when a student could still learn about God at Harvard Divinity School. Timothy had also found a job in a large, old, run-down Baptist church on Shurtleff Street, right in the heart of Chelsea, Massachusetts—the poster child of America's tough, brutal, hopeless inner cities. I worked with the preschool children in the church's basement day care program.

One hundred years before, the church had drawn the rich and privileged to worship on Sunday mornings. They had arrived in magnificent four-horse carriages where hired footmen helped Chelsea's fur-and jewel-clad elite descend to the sidewalk with pomp and circumstance.

But much had changed in Chelsea in 100 years. The run-down rock church now welcomed a handful of remnants and stragglers, and gave a home to the city's impoverished preschoolers in a makeshift basement day care center. I set up a tiny office, painted it bright yellow in an effort to overcome the sense of basement foreboding and darkness, and went to work.

Beside the church, fitting into the corner of the rock building like a puzzle piece, sat the old church parsonage. Both church and house were surrounded by an 8-foot high protective fence topped with tangled strands of barbwire. In the old days, before the fence was ever needed, the proud two-storied house watched the city's society ladies ascend the front stairs with plumed hats and white gloves, and politely sip tea with cream, and nibble on sugar-powdered crumpets. The dining room boasted of an electric lighted crystal chandelier, and the upstairs powder room prided itself with indoor plumbing. Not much had changed or been updated when Timothy and I moved into the house. Some antique crumpet plates and creamed-tea cups still sat silent in the built-in cupboard. The porcelain pieces, with their dainty sizes and delicate flower designs from a former century, seemed strangely out of place in the violent inner city. They proved a sad reminder of the city's better days, and were some of the few items street kids and gang members hadn't stolen to sell for drug money.

We were newly-weds when Timothy and I, at the tender ages of twenty-one, packed up our old green Plymouth Satellite with everything we owned and headed out of our Tennessee birth home. We had spent our last summer night in the South with my parents. Having filled our car trunk with a manual typewriter, an old sewing machine, a few dishes, our silver tea service wedding gift, and the beautiful quilt my grandmother's twin sister, Aunt Gertrude, had painstakingly stitched for us, we climbed into bed late that night. We had already said our "good-nights", and our final "good-byes", for the next day's fare-wells would've been too difficult, too painful, to say on that early August morning of our departure. At 4:30 the next morning, with sleep still in our eyes, we slipped into the old car and began the trip that would forever change our lives.

Three days later we arrived in a beautiful part of Boston, Massachusetts.

"What a lovely city!" I exclaimed to Timothy as I first took in the sights of Boston. "It's just like I imagined it would be! I know we'll love living here!"

"Yes, Denise," Timothy said. "Boston is beautiful. But you'd better prepare yourself for Chelsea. It's much different than Boston."

"But Chelsea's just a few miles from here. How can it be that different from this?" I asked.

"It's an inner city, Denise, and it's dirty and ugly, and it's home to a lot of hurting people."

"You talk as if we're moving to a ghetto, Timothy!"

When we finally pulled off the freeway and entered Chelsea's city limits, my mouth dropped open. The difference between the two cities was like day and night, white and black, clean and filthy, fine wine and sewer water, aged Cheddar cheese and processed Velveeta.

"We're here, Denise," Timothy told me. "This is our new home for the next four or five years."

"You're kidding, right? Timothy, you mean we have to live here? Are you serious?!"

"Yes, Denise, I'm dead serious."

We parked the car by the run down rock house inside the barbed wire fence. After whispering a silent prayer for protection, we got out of the car and looked around. Crowded wooden houses, dirty litter-strewn streets, loud shrieking sirens and dirty men and women sitting on curbs with hands extended met our eyes, ears, and noses.

"This looks like Alcatraz!" I cried. "I'd be afraid to leave the house! I've had enough of Chelsea, Timothy! I want to go home!"

Chelsea seemed the far end of the earth. We had never before been so far from home. It was another world—an alien world, and we knew immediately we didn't belong here. We were fish out of water trying to swim in a hostile and foreign sea.

Culture shock gripped us again that late afternoon when we walked into the local grocery store.

"Excuse me," I asked a clerk. "Could you please tell me where I can find grits?"

"Spell it!" the clerk barked.

"G-R-I-T-S," I told him. "Haven't you ever heard of g-r-i-t-s?"

He scratched his head, and looked at me for the longest time. A slow smile stretched across his face. "You're not from around here, are you?" he asked.

"No. We just drove here from Tennessee."

"Oh," he said.

"Well, if we got those g-r-i-t-s—ya'll," he chuckled, "they'd be in the foreign food section."

How we needed grits at that moment, our favorite Southern comfort food!

"We should've brought our own grits," I told Timothy as we walked to the foreign food section of the store. We searched through the stacks of packaged food with strange unrecognizable names and finally we found our grits! In the foreign food section! We knew we were out of our element then!

I decided not to ask the clerk where the o-k-r-a was.

CHAPTER 2

The Unforgettable Dinner Party

I first met Johnny Cornflakes on the evening of my first dinner party in Chelsea.

We had been in Chelsea only a few weeks when we received word that some of our Southern friends were driving up to New England to visit us. Fixing a big dinner in your home for visiting friends proved a vital and unavoidable sign of true Southern hospitality. We knew a candlelit dinner party would be expected of us, no matter where we lived, no matter how little food money we had, and no matter how high the barbed wire fence around Alcatraz was.

When I heard the news of our friends' arrival, I did what every young Southern woman would do in my present situation: I panicked. Then I cried. We were dirt poor with hardly any grocery money. Our shabby furniture was Early-Ugly. Our house was run-down, and our turn-of-the-century toilet often refused to flush.

But we had an elegant electric light chandelier hanging over our old dining room table, a set of century-old matching china, and the silver tea service gift set from our wedding.

If I had to give a dinner party in Alcatraz, I was determined I would give a dinner party in high Southern style—a dinner party my out-of-state guests would never forget!

For the next few days, I unpacked and polished the silver tea service. I carefully laid each piece of church-owned china in exactly the Amy Vanderbilt place for each guest. I stood on a tall stool and rubbed to shiny all the crystal tear-drops that hung from the chandelier.

Minutes before our dinner guests drove past the 8-foot barbed wire fence and into our driveway, I took a deep breath and said a quick prayer.

"Denise," Timothy told me, "this will be a wonderful dinner party. Everything is polished and perfect. Just relax and let's enjoy our guests."

"It's just got to be perfect," I said. "It's got to be as perfect as my mother's and my grandmother's dinner parties! I've got a heritage to uphold! And it's our very first dinner party in our new home. I just want our guests to remember this dinner party for a long time!"

Trying to swallow the huge lump in my throat, I took one last glance at the table. The table was fairly steady, but I worried about the chairs. They had been glued and re-glued too many times. They seemed too wobbly to be safe. I hoped our friends were still slim and trim. I wasn't sure how much weight the chairs could hold.

The table looked nice draped in a new white bed sheet that resembled a table cloth. Our silver tea service sparkled beneath the electric chandelier. And the food? We could afford only thin soup made with one onion, a box of cheap crackers, an industrial-sized can of baked beans, and a homemade concoction I named "sweet potato surprise." It contained one whole sweet potato and some other "surprising" ingredients. The name seemed appropriate. I just hoped no "surprise" would occur *after* my guests ate it!

"Come in," I heard Timothy say as he unlocked the front door's four padlocks and opened it to our guests.

I took a final deep breath, smoothed my long velvet skirt, and followed Timothy to the door. Together we welcomed and seated the guests around our dinner table.

"So far, so good," I thought. After the exchange of a few necessary greetings, inquiries about their families, and other expected niceties, I furrowed my brows at Timothy, the proper sign that told Timothy to stand and help me serve the soup. That's when I heard the slight creaking movement of the front door, and, with a quick glance, I noted that Timothy had forgotten to re-lock the four padlocks.

All of a sudden, before I had served the first dipper full of onion soup, the front door burst open. Our guests gasped. I froze. There, in all of his inebriated glory, stood Johnny Cornflakes, a half-emptied whisky bottle in his right hand. With a shout of happiness, and a stomach growling loudly with hunger, Johnny limped to the table and graced us with a gentleman's bow and a toothless grin.

I was too startled to move. My dog-eared *Book of Proper Etiquette and Southern Hospitality* never described a situation like this one! Unashamedly, Johnny picked up the large serving spoon with his left hand, still waving the whisky bottle in his right hand, still hollering with holy happiness, and began shoveling my "sweet potato surprise" into his wide-opened mouth. As Johnny gulped down the main course, my eyes froze big as saucers, my uplifted hand still grasping the dripping soup ladle, and my jaw dropped to my knees.

It proved a sight right out of a Stephen King novel. *The Dinner Party Nightmare!* Indeed, our guests reacted with revulsion and horror.

Timothy, however, seemed unalarmed. He gently took Johnny's arm, spoke a few kind words in his ear, and guided him to the kitchen. From the pots still hot on the stove, Timothy heaped a china plate full of food and gave it to Johnny, who sat at the kitchen table and relished his unexpected dinner.

I overhead a guest remark: "That sweet Timothy did just what Jesus would do—feed the hungry, give drink to the thirsty, invite inside the stranger..."

No one at the dinner table, however, compared my reaction to that of Jesus. When Timothy returned to the dining room, I still stood, unmoved, in my frozen position—wide-eyed, open-mouthed, and the soup ladle rattling in my hand.

"What should I do now?" I mumbled to myself.

"Well, let's eat!" Timothy said cheerfully as if nothing unusual had happened, as if my wonderfully-planned dinner party hadn't been ruined beyond repair. I knew I would never live this down.

I somehow regained a portion of my hostess dignity, and I quickly served the soup. But my hands shook and I felt rattled all the way down to my golden-slippered toes. Trying to remain calm, I moved as gracefully as I could back to my chair. I slightly lifted my long velvet skirt to sit down. But as I came down, another nightmare took place. I felt the old chair leg's glue give way, and in mid-air and falling, I could do nothing to keep my balance. I fell for fifteen long agonizing embarrassing minutes—or at least it seemed that long! Slow motion. Flailing arms and legs. A definite lack of social grace. I hit the dining room floor hard. The jolt knocked the breath out of me.

Out of the corner of one eye, I saw our dinner guests jump up from their seats to help me. I heard gasps, and then: "Denise! Are you okay?! Is anything broken?!"

I looked up from the floor into the horrified faces of my guests. My legs pointed to the ceiling like a "V". My long velvet skirt was settled somewhere up around my waist. During those embarrassing, wanting-to-die, moments, only one thought came to mind: "If only my mother could see me now!" It was the first time since our arrival in Chelsea that I was glad she lived 1,500 miles away!

The loud racket of a breaking chair, a woman hitting the floor, and a soup ladle bouncing across the wood floor, brought

Johnny Cornflakes staggering at great speed from the kitchen. Before my shocked guests could reach me, Johnny had wrapped both his food-covered hands around my waist and was tugging with all his drunken might to lift me from the floor. We had shared a feast with him that night, and he was determined to come to my rescue—my knight in shining armor, with the now-empty whisky bottle tucked under his arm.

That's when the last bit of carefully-controlled Christian compassion and southern social charm left me. I had had enough.

"Get away from me!" I shouted at Johnny. "Get away from me you smelly old drunk! This is all your fault! Just get away!"

But Johnny wouldn't be deterred. He was my hero, and his full stomach demanded he appropriately thank me. He somehow managed to lift me halfway to my feet, but in the chaos, fell and pulled me down with him. In front of our friends, Johnny and I lay sprawled together, our arms and legs intertwined, flat on the dining room floor.

"Timothy!!!" I shouted. "Help me!"

What happened at that point made Laurel and Hardy look like distinguished international dignitaries. Johnny grunted and struggled to lift me off the floor. He acted like I weighed 300 pounds! Just when he got me to my knees, his half-liter of liquor kicked in causing him to lose his balance and bring me down with him, again and again and again. Food flew, furniture overturned, dishes fell and shattered. By the time Johnny finally let loose of my middle, my blouse hung out of my skirt, my hose were snagged and sagging, one earring was missing, food filled my wild tangled hair, and my dignity was definitely destroyed.

For a split second, things got quiet. From the floor, I wiped tears from my face, and I looked up at my guests. I expected them to be as horrified as I was. I knew they were all "feeling my pain" and "suffering my agony" with me. That's when I noticed my guests' hands wrapped tightly around their mouths, their faces red, tears pouring from their eyes, their bellies vibrating with hilarity they dare not visibly express. They sat there, gazing at me, and trying hard to stifle their laughter.

I couldn't believe my eyes and ears. My perfect dinner party had become a Barnum & Bailey Circus, an evening of slap-stick comedy, a freakish side show, and I was the star performer.

That's when Timothy unintentionally let out a tiny muffled laugh. He just couldn't "hold it in" any longer. And neither could our guests. When I heard them break out into mutual uncontrolled belly-laughter, I stood up and stormed from the dining room.

"This is NOT funny, Timothy—and all the rest of you!" I shouted as I ran up the stairs. "How dare you laugh at me!!!"

Timothy followed me upstairs while our guests sat at the table unable to restrain their loud laughter. Johnny Cornflakes climbed up the table leg and ceremoniously sat at the head of the table in Timothy's chair. For the next few minutes, Johnny entertained our guests in our absence. He also finished off my "sweet potato surprise".

Upstairs in my bedroom, I sat on my bed, my face in my hands, and I cried. "Well, Timothy," I shouted through my tears. "That old drunk has ruined my dinner party! He has made me look like a clown! I hate that old man! Just get him out of my house and out of my life. I never want to see Johnny Cornflakes again!"

"Well, Denise," Timothy said and smiled. "Look on the bright side. This has definitely been a dinner party our guests will remember for a long time!"

Chapter 3

The Inner City "Armpit"

I had never seen a city like Chelsea before. Some 30,000 people lived crowded in Chelsea's confining city limits. People packed into wooden apartment buildings like baked beans in a small jar. It wasn't unusual to find a twelve-member family living in a two-room top floor apartment. Chelsea residents had little room to move and little space to breathe. Chelsea was so different from the vast, green forests and rich farmland I knew and loved.

Growing up in the suburban South, I never in my wildest dreams imagined that a city like Chelsea existed anywhere in the United States. I had been reared in a goldfish bowl, in a 1950s traditional southern family—protected, sheltered, and spoiled. Wally and Beaver Cleaver would have envied my lifestyle. I had no known needs and few unmet wants. Surrounded by acres of large hickory nut trees, green grass, and rich fertile rose gardens, I had spent my young life basking in nature's beauty and bounty. I spent the winters in my comfortable subdivision with its two-car garage and large treed back yard. Bikes, roller skates, Barbie dolls—I had everything a girl could want. I took private music lessons from Mr Bellhammer, who arrived at my house each Tuesday in his suit and tie with his briefcase filled with new crisp sheets of classical piano music. In the afternoons, I slipped into the music room and practiced cantatas by Beethoven and Chopin on my ivory-keyed mahogany piano.

I spent the summers on my grandparents' nearby farm eating homegrown garden vegetables, playing with cousins clad in freshly-ironed play clothes, and shopping for new patent leather shoes at Loveman's Department Store in downtown Rossville, Georgia.

My environment gave me lots of room to safely roam, trees to climb, roses to smell, and leisure hours to sit in neatly-mowed grass and dream the dreams that young girls dream. Little did I know that within a mere few years my life would be turned upside down and inside out, and all my familiar boundaries would be forever erased.

I once heard a resident describe Chelsea as the "armpit" of the United States. After living there, I can claim with confidence that Chelsea deserved its name. It was a terrible and violent place to live and work and raise a family. Dog droppings covered the streets, and the strong scents of old alcohol, vomit, and urine rose from the sidewalks. On hot, windless days, the smells proved unbearable.

Sunday morning smells were perhaps the worst of all. Saturday night in Chelsea was "party night" for the vagrant teenagers who roamed the streets, drained bottles of cheap whiskey, and slept in dark alleyways. On Saturday nights, I often lay in bed and listened to the sounds of empty booze bottles breaking against concrete sidewalks.

Saturday nights also brought out the street gangs and unspeakable violence. Violence had almost destroyed the city. With the necessity of padlocks and window bars, the community's residents had become prisoners in their own homes as they tried to protect themselves and their children against senseless violence. Knife fights on our front stoop were commonplace. Fortunately, during those years not too many gang members carried guns. But knives and fists proved just as deadly. Rival gangs routinely left their unfortunate victims lying in the streets to be discovered on Sunday mornings. Discarded drug needles, broken bottles, and human waste in the streets made Sunday mornings a major clean-up effort for the church's front-stairs volunteer crew before the handful of Chelsea church-goers ascended the steep sanctuary steps.

The contrast between Saturday night and Sunday morning bewildered me. Singing hymns and reciting litanies seemed to somehow redeem the reveries of the previous night. When on Sunday mornings the Chelsea church lit the one bright light in the whole city, the few sober folk who saw the light and sensed its warmth gathered like moths around its flame. The church was a small lone candle in a community of deepest darkness.

Nothing green grew in Chelsea. I remember no scenery in that concrete city. The windows of the parsonage looked directly into the windows of the apartment dwellers. The church parsonage was only one of two one-family homes in Chelsea. A moment of privacy proved a rare gift.

Chelsea also proved to be a rather dangerous firetrap. Old wooden apartment buildings, badly in need of repair, were stacked together like decks of playing cards. Fire codes were neglected with a wink and a bribe. Unchecked oil furnaces often caught fire and exploded, sending buildings up in flames and babies with life-scorched faces to hospitals for indigents. Corruption ruled the city, and no one seemed to care. Chelsea had had a major fire the century before. Only the rock church, the matching parsonage, and the elegant stone-crafted Copley Manse survived the blaze. But the tragedy had long been forgotten, and the charred ground quickly covered with shoddily-constructed matchbox apartments.

The city was never quiet, and the cacophony of sirens from fire engines and police cars never ceased day or night. Located next to Boston's Logan airport, Boeing 747s routinely descended so low over Chelsea that I could wave to the passengers. The noise from jet engines was deafening. During the rare few seconds of quietness when the sirens ceased and the planes landed, I could hear the sounds of hurt and hungry children crying for milk and mothers. And both proved to be in short supply.

CHAPTER 4

Chelsea's Prisoners

Chelsea was like a small, lone island of impoverished imprisoned people who lived surrounded by Boston's great wealth, museums, and old-world sophistication, and Cambridge's numerous institutions of higher education. The elite had long left Chelsea. And they had taken their dignity, their titles, and their old money with them. The Daughters of the American Revolution, the Harvard Club heirs, the great-great-great-grandchildren of the Mayflower pilgrims—they had gone to greener gardens, away from the smell and noise and raw violence that now ruled Chelsea.

Only one old woman from the Mayflower pilgrim clan remained in Chelsea. Mrs. Edward Rutherford Copley IV, a matron whose wide body resembled a pot roast, who dressed in female-minks, and who could no longer pry the diamond and emerald rings from her stubby fat fingers. Mrs. Copley refused to leave the house her great-grandfather had built—the thirty-eight-room stone cavern known as the Copley Mansion. She lived on the edge of town, near the hospital and some restaurants and shops. She kept one foot in Chelsea keeping up the old mansion, and the other foot in highbrow Boston society. She dressed in Victorian garb when she attended Chelsea's First Baptist Church on Shurtleff Street, her gray-streaked hair teased high into a lady's bun, a ruby broach resting on her buxom bosom. The wife of the late Mr. Edward Rutherford Copley IV, a rich Boston ship owner, Mrs. Copley carried her head and chin as high as a newly-clipped poodle as she walked around town in her long black flowing skirts. She kept a loaded revolver in her small beaded black purse, and she insisted the town's folk address her by her full name.

A century before, the wealthy Copley family had bought their own pew at the church, and each Sunday without fail, Mrs. Edward Rutherford Copley IV, deposited her ample body in that particular back pew, and allowed no one else to sit beside her. Not that anyone needed a place to sit on Sunday mornings at First Baptist Church. The cold gothic sanctuary, with its dark wood panels and large-eyed, open-mouthed gargoyles, seated a thousand parishioners, but only three stragglers, Mrs. Copley, and kind old Mrs. Bena still attended. Once in a great while Johnny Cornflakes graced the Sunday morning service with his attendance. He showed up just before the weekly offering was taken, and, usually without much success, left as impoverished as he came in. When Johnny was in attendance, Mrs. Copley often walked to the altar and herself guarded the offering plate until Johnny Cornflakes staggered out the front door. Johnny was a tough old bird, but Mrs. Copley's unblinking eagle eye could melt him and send him flying to escape her evil glare. No one cared much for Mrs. Copley—the strong defiant widow who, for emphasis and declaration, flaunted both her rings and her revolver.

Chelsea's children came in all colors, shapes, and sizes. They spoke dialects I had never heard. Outside, there were few trees to climb, few yards to play in, few streets not congested by traffic, and little money to leave Chelsea in search of greener pastures. The children roamed the dirty streets to escape the boredom and loneliness of crowded apartments, empty refrigerators, and roach-covered kitchen counters.

I'll never forget the day five-year-old David, a small Spanish boy who lived in a foster home, asked me what a flower was. He had never seen a real flower push its way through soil and bloom. Chelsea had no flowers and little soil in the city to grow them. It was not unusual for a child to live his entire life in Chelsea, grow up, raise a family, and never see a flower garden.

Johnny Cornflakes was the first alcoholic I had ever met. He slept under apartment porches, roamed the dirty streets looking for "valuable" garbage, and occasionally ate the leftovers that Grady and other local restaurant owners tossed out to him. As far as Johnny Cornflakes was concerned, Grady served up a king's banquet back there in the dirty alley behind the diner.

No one seemed to know anything about Johnny's past, where he came from, who he was. No one except Mrs. M. H. Bena. And she wasn't talking. An occasional Cornflakes-inquiry usually left a Mona Lisa smile on Mrs. Bena's wrinkled face and a slight twinkle in her eye. Whatever she knew in her heart about Johnny Cornflakes, stayed there.

Come to think of it, no one knew much about Mrs. Bena either. She came to church faithfully every Sunday morning, sat with some street urchins she gathered up before the service, and always smelled like vanilla flavoring. She had the finely-chiseled chin and high cheekbones of Early American aristocracy, but, unlike Mrs. Copley, she wore no bejeweled advertisements of wealth or position. Mrs. Bena wore dark-colored, heavy woolen suits from Zurich, 1940, and sturdy flat shoes with tire-tread soles. The elderly widow lived in a first-floor apartment in the heart of Chelsea, next to the tire factory and city dump, and kept her door always open for those who needed a listening ear or a fresh-from-the-oven chocolate chip cookie. She was tight-lipped, but smiling, when asked to respond to an occasional random rumor about a Swiss bank account and a family-owned mountain chalet high above Lucerne's art-covered bridges. Sometimes she offered a soft answer, "Those things don't mean anything to me anymore."

During our sojourn in Chelsea, I shared many a cookie with Mrs. Bena in her tiny kitchen with the brown bottles of sweet vanilla lined up in the window above her sink. And every once in a while, I'd see a far-away look in her eye. And if I stopped talking and closely listened, she would tell me about Chelsea's long-gone high society, concerts in the city's parks, and Sunday after church strolls with her handsome, unnamed gentleman friend as they walked arm in arm beneath her lace-trimmed parasol.

"I've heard Chelsea referred to as the nation's 'armpit'," I once told Mrs. Bena. "It was quite a shock to me when I first came to this dirty, nasty city. And I have nothing in common with all these dirty...ah...ah...I mean 'unfortunate' people."

"Yes," she replied. "But even dirty, unfortunate, 'armpit' people are precious to God."

I later learned that Mrs. Bena's grandfather helped build the grand old Chelsea church where my young student-husband served as pastor. He had painstakingly placed the hand-cut rock, helped design the stain glass windows, and had overseen the construction of the tall cross-shaped steeple. That was, of course, in those vibrant and young years before the down-and-outers, the transients, the homeless and the hopeless of Chelsea had settled there and claimed the motto: "Abandon hope, all ye who enter here."

It was in this hostile setting that Timothy and I lived, worked, loved, and learned. For a southern girl used to a fine lifestyle, Chelsea proved disgusting—the city and the people. I didn't want to stay. I lay in bed at night and dreamed of going back home where "decent" people lived and order ruled. I hated this place. During those first few months in Chelsea, I felt miserable, homesick and afraid—and with good reason.

CHAPTER 5

The Crypts

I held my nose as I walked toward the parsonage, away from Mrs. Bena's home, the tire factory, and the city dump. I longed for the gentle fresh breezes that floated from pine-tree covered Lookout Mountain near my Tennessee home.

When I crossed Shurtleff Street, I saw a group of tough-looking guys, twelve males between the ages of about 16 to 21. I had been warned about them. They were violent and dangerous. Called themselves "The Crypts." Knife was their leader.

That's when the cat-calls began.

"Chihuahua!! Look at what just moved into the neighborhood!" Knife, the leader of the Crypts gang shouted.

"Hey gorgeous," he called. "What's your name? C'mon honey. Speak to me. Let me get a better look at you!"

"Leave me alone!" I shouted as I reached the parsonage's front gate. With shaking hands, I unlocked the padlock with my key, fell inside, and quickly relocked the gate.

"It's okay, good lookin'," he hollered. "Like the song says: 'time is on my side'. We'll get to know each other real well. I promise!"

I ran inside my house, locked the doors, checked all the window locks, and sat down on the floor, breathed deeply, and tried to control my fear. An hour later, when I heard no more laughter and cat-calls and threats, I stood up, looked out the window, and said a prayer of thanksgiving that they were gone and I was inside and okay.

Later that evening, I told Timothy about the scary experience.

"Some gang members called the Crypts said some obscene things to me today. They really scared me. I think they might have tried to hurt me if they could've."

"Yeah, I've heard about the Crypts. Dangerous youth gang. You need to stay away from them, Denise."

"Timothy, why did you bring me to Chelsea? Why can't we live in Boston or Cambridge like all the other Harvard students, and be safe?"

"Because I made a commitment, Denise. I offered to minister to the people here and to pastor the church. Anyway, we need the money for tuition, even if it's just a small amount."

"Why can't you get a job on campus, in the cafeteria, or the bookstore, instead of in Chelsea? It'd pay just about as much."

"Because, Denise, I've been 'called' to ministry—to do God's work. And it looks like there's a lot of people here in Chelsea who desperately need ministry and help."

"Well, Timothy, maybe you've been 'called', but I haven't heard any voice from heaven calling ME to do ministry here! Why should I suffer, be afraid, and live like this when God 'called' YOU to Chelsea?! It sure doesn't seem very fair to me!"

"I understand how you feel, Denise."

"Well, Timothy, just don't expect much help from me during the next five years! I'm not even going to unpack the dishes. I want to go home! I'll be lucky if I just get out of Chelsea alive!"

Late that night, I slipped out of bed and got down on my knees.

"God!" I prayed. "Why did You bring me to this horrible place? What did I do to deserve this? I want to go home, God! What can anybody possibly do anyway to help these people? Why do You even want us to help them? They're disgusting. They're dirty. Most of them are lying in the streets drunk. Whatever are they good for? Whatever can anyone do to help them?!"

With the prayer on my lips, and with disgust and hatred in my heart, I sobbed myself to sleep that night. I wondered how I could stand, how I could endure, one more day in this prison.

CHAPTER 6

The Coffee House

In order to attract Chelsea's young people to the church, Timothy started an open-door Coffee House on Friday nights in the church basement. He offered music, games, soft drinks, and potato chips. Mrs. Bena added homemade sugar cookies to our menu. That usually proved enough encouragement to bring in transient and troubled teens. When the potato chips and sugar cookies ran out, Timothy invited the teens to a brief Bible study. After a few weeks, we had a handful of regular attendees.

One Friday night, Mrs. Copley attended the Coffee House.

"Pastor George," she said as she stood with her bejeweled hands on her wide hips. "This is a church! It is not a place to serve food and entertain the city's teenaged scum!"

"Mrs. Copley," Timothy said. "After we eat some snacks, we read the Bible and pray together. I'm trying to teach these teens about God's love for them."

"So," said Mrs. Copley. "You think God actually loves these trouble-makers? If He loves them so much, why doesn't He take better care of them—feed them, protect them, help them become worthwhile citizens?!"

"Scripture tells us that their Heavenly Father loves them, and that's what they need to know, Mrs. Copley."

"Well," Mrs. Copley said as she turned to leave. "I'll have no part of it! And I'll be putting nothing in the offering plate as long as this Coffee House fiasco continues!"

"Before you go, Mrs. Copley, won't you have one of Mrs. Bena's sugar cookies?" Lisa asked her.

"Well, I do have a sweet tooth. Yes, thank you," said Mrs. Copley and crammed two cookies in her purse. "But I will eat them outside the walls of the church!" she spat.

Mrs. Bena sat quietly in the back of the basement, slightly shaking her head from side to side, a smile on her face, her lips moving in silent prayer. The large thick stick she used as a walking cane lay beside her.

"I'll make up the difference in the offering," she later told Timothy. "If Mrs. Copley stops tithing, I'll contribute her part to the church's operating budget. You just keep doing what you're doing for our city's young people!"

We had a small core of "regulars" who came faithfully every Friday night. Most had had tragic pasts, but through this study, each was finding a new faith in a loving Father. Their lives were taking on new meaning and new exuberance as they embraced their Heavenly Father's love.

The teens were a most unusual group of people. *Weird* might be a better word to describe them. Lisa and Jenny had run away from troubled homes as young teens. Rick had been addicted to heroin and various other illegal drugs. Sam grew up in an abusive foster home, ran away at age fourteen, and ended up in prison for theft. Jason had been a gang member with the Crypts. Paul had been mixed up with a drug dealer. We found him lying on the church steps one Sunday morning, unconscious and badly-beaten.

The teens came to form a tight-knit group. They supported and encouraged each other. They shared clothes and food and helped each other find places to live. They were each different from the other, yet they had so much in common. They had known street life and had learned to fight and survive in a hostile environment. They were tough kids who wore torn jeans (before they became popular), oversized t-shirts, and army surplus combat boots. They wore their hair long and their clothes tattered. They had no money, but they enjoyed a mysterious type of sweet Christian joy that I had yet to discover.

They also invited other street kids to study God's Word during the Friday night Coffee House times.

"Your earthly father might not be around," I heard Jason tell a newcomer teen. "But your Heavenly Father is always with you."

"Mrs. Bena is the best," they also told the wary visitors. "She brings us cookies, and slips dollar bills in our hands if she thinks we look hungry."

"But," they always added, "Watch out for Mrs. Copley. She packs lead! Don't mess with her!"

Timothy fit in nicely with Chelsea's young people. He left his "clean-cut" look back in Tennessee and let his light brown hair grow past his ears and spill onto his collar. He also stopped shaving and allowed a bushy beard to take over his face. The first day we arrived in Chelsea, he donned overalls and boots, rolled up his shirt sleeves, and went to work. The teens loved Timothy and claimed him as one of their own.

I, however, chose to bring my southern culture with me to Chelsea. No way would I wear overalls and work boots, not even when I worked with Chelsea's preschoolers in our church's day care. I stuck to my bounces and flounces and bows in my hair. I definitely did not "fit in."

Nor did I want to.

Chapter 7

My Second Meeting with Johnny Cornflakes

On one rather unremarkable Friday night, I again encountered Johnny Cornflakes. Our little group of faithful "regulars" met as usual in the church basement for Mrs. Bena's cookies and Bible study. We formed a small circle with metal folding chairs, opened our Bibles, and began our study.

"Sam," Timothy asked. "Would you please read from Matthew 25?"

Sam fumbled through his Bible. He had never read Matthew before and had no idea where the book was located in the Bible.

"It's in the New Testament, the first book," Timothy gently told him. I sighed a loud breath of pure impatience as I waited for Sam to find what I considered the easiest book in the entire Bible to find. For a full five minutes, Sam thumbed through his Bible trying to locate the Gospel of Matthew. When he finally found it, he began to read, slowly and carefully, one word at a time. He stopped from time to time and looked up at Timothy. Timothy nodded his encouragement, a sort of "you're doing great, Sam", and Sam continued to read. Sam had long before dropped out of school and even simple reading proved difficult for him. But his zeal and enthusiasm for his newfound faith more than made up for his lack of reading skills.

I knew the passage in Matthew 25 forwards and backwards. In fact, I knew it so well that it held little meaning for me anymore. While Sam read, my thoughts drifted back to my grandparents' farm and Inky the pony, Little Man the dog, and the afternoon watermelon slicings for the grandchildren.

It took a long time, but Sam continued to read. "For I was hungry and you gave me something to eat, I was thirsty and you gave me something to drink, I was a stranger and you invited me in, I needed clothes and you clothed me, I was sick and you looked after me, I was in prison and you came to visit me."

Sam stopped reading. His face turned crimson and in his young heart a light came on as he lifted tired eyes and looked into the faces of those sitting around him, those who had known hunger and thirst, who had been sick and addicted, who had needed clothes, who had been unwanted strangers, who had been in prison.

He wiped his eyes with his sleeve, and after a long moment, he continued reading. "Lord, when did we see you hungry and feed you, or thirsty and give you something to drink? When did we see you a stranger and invite you in, or needing clothes and clothe you? When did we see you sick or in prison and go to visit you?"

"I tell you the truth," Sam continued reading, "whatever you did for one of the least of these brothers of mine, you did for me."

The little group sat very still and quiet after Sam stopped reading. Most had not heard these words before and they had much to ponder. They knew firsthand what it meant to be hungry, naked, sick, and imprisoned. The expressions on their faces showed they needed some time to digest what Sam had just read to them.

For a long time that night the group talked with Timothy about the meaning of "the least of these" and our responsibility to those who are needy, to those we call "neighbor". I must admit that while the group pondered the Scriptures, I allowed my thoughts to continue to float 1,500 miles away. "Oh, I miss home so much," I inwardly moaned. "Why did we ever leave the South to come to this god-forsaken place? How I hate this city with its dirt and its crime and its disgusting people."

Before I could continue my inward complaining, however, the basement door burst open. A cold October wind blasted the room, wildly flipping Bible pages.

Johnny Cornflakes staggered inside. He wore a navy blue suit, twenty years out of style and covered with city dirt. Wisps of white hair danced around his face—a face carved by years of hard drinking and hostile New England winters.

With stooped shoulders and an age-etched frown, he resembled a Ringling Brother's circus clown as he limped into the room. He proceeded to step on eight pairs of feet only to land, amazingly, upright in the chair next to mine. Once seated, he turned his entire body toward me and with large bloodshot eyes gazed into my face.

Still staring at me, Johnny opened his food-encrusted, toothless mouth and smiled. The stench of body odor and alcohol hit me full force. I jerked my head away and wrapped my hand tightly over my face. My stomach reeled. I thought I would be sick.

"Excuse me!" I said, jumping up, my hand still tightly wrapped around my mouth. I headed for the ladies room down the hall. For a full ten minutes, I hung my head over the sink, breathed deeply, splashed cold water on my face, and struggled to keep back the nausea.

When I reentered the room and sat down in my chair, I longed with every part of my being to be back home with the people I knew and loved. I felt large, hot tears run along the rims of my eyelids.

How I intensely disliked this place. How I loathed the old man who sat beside me in the worn-out suit, who smelled bad, and who staggered his way through life.

As I sat in the Bible study and eyed Johnny, I thought to myself, "Johnny, isn't it enough that you ruined my dinner party, and embarrassed me to death? Must you now follow me into my church, plop down beside me, and breathe your awful whiskey breath in my face?"

Johnny noticed my unblinking glare, turned his head to me, and again smiled. I narrowed my eyes into evil slits and gave him my best "mad dog" look. "How dare he come into God's House all liquored up!" I thought. "How dare he intrude on my study of God's Word!"

CHAPTER 8

Johnny's Shoe

Vividly remembering the dinner party Johnny had ruined, I sat stiffly in the metal chair glaring at the old man while the others sat quietly, still focused on the meaning of Matthew 25. Johnny's body odor was unbearable. I put my hand to my nose and tried not to breathe. I looked around the room to see how the rest of the group was bearing the stench. That's when I noticed all eyes focused on Johnny's shoe. I saw it too. His twisted mass of un-socked foot, crippled by a childhood disease, was stuffed into an over-sized shoe with a large gaping hole in the toe. Johnny had pushed cardboard into the hole, trying to shut out the blustery New England winter.

Jason broke the uncomfortable silence. "You know, it won't be long till winter snow comes," he said. "I think Jesus would want us to buy Johnny another shoe." The others agreed and immediately emptied their pockets. Jason counted out $15.53 worth of dimes, nickels, and quarters.

"This should be more than enough for a shoe," he guessed. "Let's get Johnny to the foot doctor tomorrow."

I couldn't believe my ears. They were actually going to spend their money on a shoe for Johnny!

"Well, I believe in helping the poor, but aren't there agencies that could give Johnny a shoe?" I asked.

"With all the papers and red tape," Lisa piped in, "it will be next summer before Johnny gets a shoe." At that point, I decided to keep quiet. I silently wished Mrs. Copley had joined us that evening. She would have definitely backed me up.

Money was so scarce in Chelsea that we, ourselves, could hardly buy groceries. I hadn't had a new pair of shoes in a year. I still wore last year's shoes, and they were horribly out of style. But if they wanted to spend $15.53 on a shoe for Johnny, I would keep my mouth shut. And I certainly wouldn't be giving any of my money to help buy it.

I glanced back at Mrs. Bena. She had a smile on her face and tears in her eyes, and she stayed strangely silent. *Why doesn't Mrs. Bena offer some money for the shoe?* I wondered. *Hadn't I heard she had a Swiss bank account and a chalet in Lucerne?* To my surprise, no one in the group asked Mrs. Bena to contribute to Johnny's shoe fund.

The next day Timothy and Rick took Johnny to the foot doctor. "Johnny's foot is so badly deformed," the doctor explained, "a new shoe designed to fit him will cost $113.92."

"One hundred thirteen dollars and ninety-two cents?!" I shouted when I heard the price of the new shoe. "No one in our little group has ever seen that much money all at once! There's no way we can buy that shoe! Johnny'll just have to live with cardboard in his sole!"

The next Friday night, we told the Coffee House group about the shoe and the money it would cost.

"Since we can't buy the shoe," I suggested, "let's use the money we've collected for something else."

But Rick and the others wouldn't hear of it. "Johnny needs that shoe," he said. "Anyway," he asked, and looked me squarely in the eye, "isn't Johnny one of the 'least of these' that Jesus talks about?"

My face turned red, and I said nothing else.

"We'll just have to somehow earn the money for Johnny's shoe!" Rick stated. The other teens agreed, said a final closing prayer asking God to provide them with paying jobs around town, and left the church.

CHAPTER 9

Going to Work

The next morning, Lisa, Jenny, Rick, Sam, Jason, and Paul hit the streets of Chelsea in search of odd jobs. I watched them hard at work as I walked around town. They picked up trash, moved furniture, washed windows, and cleaned local store floors. Coming out of the post office, I ran into Mrs. Copley.

"Good morning, Mrs. George," she said. "I hope you're having a good day."

"Thank you, Mrs. Copley," I replied. "But I've had better days."

"What do you mean?" she asked.

"Our Bible study teens are trying to earn money to buy Johnny Cornflakes a new shoe to fit his deformed foot. They are all over town doing odd jobs to make enough money for it."

"Why would they want to do that for that old drunk who sleeps in the gutters and eats food out of the city trash cans?" she asked.

"I honestly don't know, Mrs. Copley."

"Well, I certainly won't give any of my money to the fund!" she quipped. "And I won't give them any work to do to earn it either!"

Then, with a laugh, Mrs. Copley made a suggestion. "Why don't you ask old Mrs. Margaret Bena for the money? She's certainly the bleeding heart type. But I doubt she could give you much money. It's such a shame the woman couldn't manage her financial affairs better."

Later that afternoon, I walked to Mrs. Bena's apartment. My conversation with Mrs. Copley had strangely unsettled my stomach. It left an odd taste in my mouth. I needed to talk to Mrs. Bena about these unusual feelings I felt.

I knocked on the door several times, but no one answered. I walked around to the back of her apartment building, the side nearest the city dump, but she wasn't outside. I waited a few minutes and hoped she would return. That's when I saw an old woman standing in the middle of the dump. She carried a large burlap sack over one shoulder, and every few seconds, she bent down to the ground to pick something up and toss it in the sack. *Who is she?* I wondered. *What in the world is she doing?*

Lisa skipped by and interrupted my thoughts.

"Hi Denise!" she said. "Did you come to see Mrs. Bena?"

"Yes," I told Lisa. "But she's not home. I really need to talk with her."

"There she is," Lisa said and pointed to the dump. "That's Mrs. Bena."

"What in the world is she doing?" I asked.

"Oh, she's picking up tin cans that restaurants have thrown in the dump," Lisa said. "The factory down the street pays her two cents a can for the scrap tin. In fact, I came over today to help her. Want to help us?"

I blinked a few times and tried to focus my eyes on the old woman who stood in the middle of the city dump.

"I thought Mrs. Bena had money!" I said abruptly. "Doesn't she have money in Switzerland and a house in Lucerne … or something like that?"

"She used to," Lisa stated matter of fact. "But she doesn't anymore. She sold the house and gave all her money away."

"She gave it all away?" I echoed.

"That's right. Why do you think she lives in this shabby little apartment by the dump?" Lisa asked me. "And why do you think she picks up tin cans at the dump to buy sugar and flour and flavoring to make cookies for the Bible study kids?"

"Who'd she give her money to?" I asked.

"Whoever needed it," Lisa answered. "I asked her one time why she lived in Chelsea and not in Back Bay Boston? She told me she couldn't afford to live in Back Bay, and anyway, she didn't want to. She loved the people in Chelsea. She also told me something I'll never forget as long as I live. She said: 'Lisa, fortunes are meant to be invested in people, not in things.' Mrs. Bena has supported about half the residents of Chelsea at one time or another. She also gave the money to open the church's child day care so single moms could find jobs. When Dad went to prison, and Mom became addicted to drugs, Mrs. Bena rented an apartment for Jenny and me. She bought our groceries, gave us warm coats for the winter, and had our cavities filled at her own dentist's office."

Mrs. Bena and Lisa picked up 50 tin cans that day and donated their hard-earned dollar to the "Johnny Cornflakes Shoe Fund." The rest of the teens worked odd jobs for six weeks until they finally earned $113.92—to the penny. And they bought Johnny's shoe.

CHAPTER 10

The Search for Johnny

It was snowing the next Friday night as we admired the new shoe and waited at the church for Johnny. One hour, two hours, three hours crept by. But Johnny didn't come.

"Do you think he's left town?" Paul asked.

"Maybe he's sick somewhere, or even … dead," Jenny said.

I could stand it no longer. "The old drunk!" I blurted out. "He could at least show up and get his new shoe!"

Then Rick spoke. "Well, we'll just have to go out and find Johnny and take the shoe to him."

"It's not safe to be on the streets this time of night," I warned them. "What if we run into the Crypts?"

But they were determined. So I decided to tag along. I followed the small group from behind. Because it was wet and dirty, I didn't want to join them in the search. But old Mrs. Bena, supported by her stick-cane, helped them search for Johnny, and I felt like I should go too.

We walked around Chelsea for the next few hours as Mrs. Bena and the teenagers crawled under apartment porches, checked out local restaurant alleys, searched the city's trash bins, and combed the filthy streets calling Johnny's name.

When they finally emerged from their search, they looked worse than I imagined Johnny himself looked. City grime covered their hands, feet, and even their faces, and mud clung to their clothes. They looked a mess. Even Mrs. Bena had mud speckled on her glasses. And they still hadn't found Johnny. They finally gave up the search, and we all headed back to the church.

Several days passed. We had a treasure in our midst, a hard-earned treasure worth $113.92. We walked the streets of Chelsea, looking for Johnny, and carrying the expensive shoe in the same way the handsome Prince hunted for Cinderella to fit her foot into the famed glass slipper.

Sam had been entrusted to "keep the shoe" while we searched day after day for Johnny Cornflakes. But after several weeks of calling out his name and searching for him in the city's back alleys, we finally gave up. Week after week, as our little group carried the shoe to each Bible study, hoping Johnny would show up, we lost a little more hope of ever finding him.

Johnny was gone. He had vanished into thin air.

And we were left with an expensive shoe that would only fit Johnny's twisted foot.

Chapter 11

The Break-In

On the last Friday night in November, we wrapped the shoe in tissue paper and placed it back in its box. Sam tied twine tightly around the large white box, put it under his arm, and took it to his home to keep it safe until the group could decide what to do with it.

Timothy had planned an out-of-town mission trip on the following night. We spent Saturday morning washing clothes, packing, and counting pocket change to meet his travel expenses.

As he always did when he traveled, Timothy left me plenty of safety instructions.

"Lock the doors, Denise, and check the windows to make sure they're locked, too," he said.

I didn't like the idea of spending Saturday night, or any night, alone in the two-story house, but there was nothing I could do about it. We had been in Chelsea long enough to have had everything we owned stolen. Break-in after break-in had robbed us of everything we owned, with the exception of the silver tea service (which I kept well-hidden), a new pair of twin bed sheets, and Aunt Gertrude's handmade quilt. Our old manual typewriter was even stolen during one of the many robberies. Fortunately, thieves chose to rob us when we were away from home. Only one time did I enter the back door of the parsonage while a young thief quickly exited the house through the front door.

After each robbery, we called the police. Often it took two or three calls before the police came. On several occasions the police never came at all. We always filed the necessary reports, knowing however that little would be done to find the crook or to prevent the next break-in.

And the thieves were growing bolder. They now came in through the padlocked front door in broad daylight. They broke windowpanes and made little effort to hide their intended robbery.

"Be careful," Timothy told me as he slipped into his coat, stepped into the deep snow on that cold November morning, and began his trek to the car. "I'll be back tomorrow."

That night, I carefully checked the first- and second-story windows to make sure they were securely locked. I fastened the front door padlocks and checked the back door's bolt. All seemed secure enough. But Saturday night was no night to take chances, so I rechecked all the locks before I changed into my nightgown and climbed into bed.

From my bed, I could see out the second-story window. It was a clear night. The tall street lamp next to our house showed the streets to be less crowded on this Saturday night than usual. It seemed strange, like some sort of "calm" before the storm. I looked forward to a good night's sleep. Sleep was the one way I could escape the horrors of the inner city. When I closed my eyes in sleep, I could be instantly transported anywhere I wanted to go.

And I most wanted to go home.

I could pretend I was a little girl again back on my grandparents' farm where Mama's lovely flowers bloomed and hickory nut trees grew straight and tall. Their farm had been my summer paradise. Mornings brought gentle rains. Afternoons brought chicken frying in cast-iron skillets, pound cakes cooling on the counter, fried okra, garden corn still on the ear and dripping with butter, and homemade biscuits baking in the oven.

My grandparents never had a lot of money, but Mama always made sure each of her six visiting grandchildren had a dime in hand when the ice cream truck stopped in front of the old white gabled house.

Sleep brought thoughts of Mama and long-ago, faraway memories I thought I had forgotten. As sleep came that late Saturday night, I dreamt about Mama and what I most loved about her. She had a heart of gold. She was a kind and giving woman who loved people and made sure she delivered a big jar of homemade vegetable soup to anyone who fell sick.

In a way, she reminded me of dear old Mrs. Bena with her stick-cane and her empty bank accounts. And the smile that always adorned her face.

I remembered the summer day a little barefoot girl in a torn, dirty dress knocked on Mama's front door. Mama invited her inside. She was about my age, but she didn't look like any of my friends or me. In her small hands, she held some ragged dish towels.

"Would you like to buy some of these?" she timidly asked my grandmother.

Mama smiled. "I sure would! How did you know just exactly what I needed?!" Mama went to her secret place where her coins were hidden, and when she returned, I watched her slip a generous handful of coins into the girl's dress pocket.

"I'll buy one dishtowel," she told the girl, "and the rest of the money is for you."

I never forgot Mama's kindness to the girl.

Before long, sleep took over, and I gladly relinquished my cherished memories for a needed night's rest. I knew Timothy would arrive very early the next morning to clean the church steps and get everything ready for Sunday's church service.

I had become quite accustomed to the routine Saturday night noises. Even though tonight seemed quieter than most Saturday nights, planes still dipped into the neighboring airport, fire engines continued to scream and race up and down Chelsea's narrow streets, and drunken kids still threw empty liquor bottles against distant city buildings. But those noises didn't usually keep me awake anymore.

Something happened, however, about three o'clock that morning that made me suddenly sit straight up in bed. I turned my head and stopped breathing to listen to the unusual sounds.

Voices. I could hear voices, not loud drunken voices, but voices speaking in whispers. I slipped out of bed and knelt by the window. Trying not to be seen, I peeked out and saw a sight that made my heart stop.

A dozen Crypt gang members stood on the sidewalk under my bedroom window. One by one they climbed over the eight-foot fence with its tangled sharp barbed wire top, and crept quietly into our yard.

In their hands, they carried crowbars, making it clear what they intended to do. They didn't see our green Plymouth Satellite in the driveway and assumed no one was home. I knew they planned to break in through a window and rob the house. My mind raced. I had remembered to lock all the windows on the first and second floor. But the garage room window that led to the basement? Had I remembered to lock it? I couldn't remember. We used that room for storage, and I hadn't been in that part of the house for a long time.

"Be calm, Denise," I told myself again and again. I made my way across the room to the telephone and dialed the police.

"Officer, please send someone to 27 Bellingham Street, on the corner of Shurtleff Street! The Crypts gang members are trying to break into my house!" I cried.

I hung up the receiver and held my breath, hoping the police would hurry. I had no gun, no knife, no protection whatsoever in the house. Up against so many violent teens, I knew I couldn't defend myself.

"Hurry, please hurry," I cried under my breath and listened for the police car siren. From the window, I watched the rest of the gang jump over the barbed wire fence. They had discovered the garage room window. I could hear the scratch of the crowbar as they forced it under the window.

"Hurry!" I cried as I redialed the police. "Please, officer! They are breaking into my window! I'm here by myself! Hurry! Please hurry!"

I knelt down by the window and silently prayed for God's protection. That's when I heard the window pop. It was locked, but the lock had given way to the crowbar. With others still jumping over the fence, I could hear the sickening sound of the window opening. I waited breathlessly for the police, but heard no siren. I only heard the sound of strong young bodies lifting themselves into the house through the garage room window. I raced to my bedroom door and firmly fastened the lock. I knew it wouldn't be long now before they found the stairs and bounded up to my bedroom.

I wondered: *What will I do? What will I say? How can I protect myself from this dangerous gang?* I remembered Knife's cat-call to me in the street: "It's okay, good lookin'," he had hollered. "Like the song says: 'time is on my side'. We'll get to know each other real well. I promise!"

Suddenly, a strange voice from under my bedroom window called out: "No! No! You can't go in there!"

I searched the yard. No, it wasn't the police. Again I heard the voice yelling: "Go away! Go away!"

What I heard next sounded like a hard punch to someone's stomach and the sound of gasping and falling. Whoever had been hit in the gut was still calling out in a pained voice: "No! You can't go in there!"

In the midst of the stranger's painful heaving and gagging, I heard another loud scream. A blood-curdling, bone-chilling scream, sharp and raw with fear and pain.

"Help me! Help me! I'm hurt!" the young voice cried out.

One of the last gang members to climb over the fence had caught his knee in the jagged barbed wire on top. His flesh was torn to the bone, hanging from his leg, and his pants were soaked in blood.

Writhing in pain and unable to free himself from the sharp barbed wire, he screamed wildly for his buddies. At that moment, the entire Crypt gang turned and stormed out of my house, their attention directed immediately to their injured friend. It took the whole lot of them to untangle his flesh and lift him down to the ground.

"He needs a doctor!" Knife shouted. One of the teens hot-wired a parked van nearby. They lifted the crying youth into the stolen van, jumped in beside him, and with a loud screech of tires, took off for the hospital.

It took me several minutes to realize what had just happened. I was in shock. They were gone—all of them. But I was too afraid to go downstairs. For the longest time, I sat on the floor staring out my bedroom window and thanking God for His divine and timely intervention.

And as I prayed, I noticed a shadowy figure emerge from beneath my bedroom window.

"Oh, no!" I cried and caught my breath. Someone was still down there. I watched the figure as he tried several times to stand up. Heaving, he headed away from my house, his left hand clutching his stomach, his right hand raised to his head.

"Who?" I whispered to myself. "Who are you?"

As the mysterious figure moved toward the street lamp, I noticed a familiar limp.

"Johnny? Johnny Cornflakes?! Is it you, Johnny?!" I whispered.

Directly under the light, I watched the old man's white wispy hair dance as the cold November winds blew all around him. And I saw one noticeably large misshaped shoe print in the snow.

CHAPTER 12

Johnny Cornflakes—My Hero?!

I had quite a story to tell Timothy when he returned later that morning. I still couldn't believe Johnny Cornflakes had been the loud voice I heard, that he had tried to protect me from the Crypts, and that he had taken a blow to the stomach on my behalf.

I realized that Johnny's actions did not in the least deter the teens, but he had tried to protect me. I shuddered when I realized the gang members could have killed the tired old man.

The next Friday night I could hardly wait to tell the Bible study teens that Johnny Cornflakes was alive, that I had seen him the week before! As we took our places in the cold metal chairs, I recited to them the horrors of the past Saturday night.

"Did the police ever come?" they asked me.

"No, they never came, even though I called them several times," I answered.

"Are you sure the stranger was Johnny Cornflakes?" they asked.

"Yes, I'm positive it was Johnny. I recognized his limp. I saw him under the street lamp. I know it was Johnny. Anyway," I added, "I'd certainly recognize that big, ugly shoe he drags along!"

"Did the Crypts hurt Johnny?" they wanted to know.

"I'm sure they hurt him. He fell to the ground, and he held his stomach when he finally stood up."

"Where did Johnny go?"

"I have no idea where he went after that," I said. "I haven't seen him all week."

After all the questions had been asked and answered, a pained look crossed Paul's face.

"You know, Denise," he said, "it takes a brave man to do what Johnny did for you last Saturday night. He could have been killed. The Crypts have killed others in Chelsea. Johnny must really care about you to risk his life to try to save yours."

I burrowed my brows, and thought for a long moment about the possibility that had never occurred to me. *Could Johnny Cornflakes really care about me? I silently pondered. I have never said a kind word to Johnny. I have done nothing but insult the old man. How could he possibly care about me?*

"Do you really think he cares about me?" I asked Paul.

"I don't know, Denise," he answered, "but he cared enough to try to protect you against a whole gang, didn't he?" Then Paul added: "I think I might even call that 'love'!"

That comment went straight to my heart. It remained my constant thought for the following two weeks. *Why had Johnny risked his life to protect me? I wondered. Could it really be true? Could he actually care about me?* I had never considered myself anything to Johnny but an occasional free lunch that I hatefully handed out the back door to bribe him to leave my yard. *Love? Johnny Cornflakes, capable of love?*

That week I finally decided to unpack my dishes. Even though I longed to go back home to the South, it looked like we would be staying in Chelsea for a while. As I placed the cups and saucers inside the kitchen cabinets, I thought about Johnny's heroic deed. And I began to wonder about the old man who kept a bottle of cheap liquor by his side and who stumbled through the streets of the dirty city I was finally – reluctantly – beginning to call "home".

CHAPTER 13

Preparing for Christmas

I worked hard during those next few weeks before Christmas. The children in the church basement daycare had definitely caught the Christmas spirit. Everything seemed magical to them during the Christmas season. They loved the music, the lights, and the falling snow. When Paul dressed up in borrowed Santa garb and surprised us with a visit, each child sat on his lap and rattled off his or her Christmas wish list.

"Ho! Ho! Ho! What do you want for Christmas?" Paul asked Mitchell, a thin Spanish boy.

"I want a bicycle and a baseball bat," Mitchell answered, and then added: "And I want my daddy to come see me."

Michelle's wish was similar. "I want my mommy to be well again and I want us to always have enough food to eat."

By the time little Rachel climbed upon Santa's red-velvet lap, tears were forming in Paul's eyes. "I want my mommy to get off drugs and come back home to me," the small girl cried.

Christmastime brought rare smiles to the faces of the city's preschoolers. They decorated the halls of the daycare with handmade reindeer and pictures of wreaths of green holly and red berries. The crayoned pictures on the walls told the stories of these young children—the victims of Chelsea's crime and poverty. They showed dogs and cats, brothers and sisters, a mother and a grandmother, standing by a lopsided Christmas tree. Never in their pictures did I see a father, nor did I ever see a brother older than sixteen. It seemed that young fathers and older brothers didn't stay long inside the family structures. Fragmented families were one of the many tragedies of inner-city life. Somehow, with little means, the women kept the families together and saved enough money to provide a meager Christmas for the children.

With the hard work of Christmas before me, I didn't think much about Johnny Cornflakes anymore. I hadn't seen him since the break-in incident.

One afternoon, as I made my way to the post office in knee-high snow to mail a handful of Christmas cards, I caught sight of a stooped-over, white-haired man in a weathered navy suit.

"Johnny!" I called to the man and raced through the snow to reach him. "Johnny, I just want to thank you for..." I cut my statement short when the old man turned around and gave me a puzzled stare.

"I'm so sorry, sir. I thought you were someone else," I apologized and turned away.

As I walked through the falling snow toward home, I began to wonder more deeply about this character we called Johnny Cornflakes.

"Just who are you?" I asked myself aloud as I turned onto Shurtleff Street. "Where did you come from? Do you have a home? A family? How did you end up living on the streets of Chelsea? Where do you go when the outside temperature drops below freezing?"

For some unknown reason, I had the strange desire to know more about this man who had stuck out his neck (or rather, his stomach) on my behalf that Saturday night when I was frightened out of my wits.

At least I owed him a proper "thank you" for trying to help me. Anyway, six concerned teenagers were daily searching the streets for him; everywhere they went, they carried the new shoe in their hands. At least if I could find him, they could give him his shoe.

But where would I start looking for Johnny Cornflakes—the old weathered man who kept a bottle of cheap liquor by his side and who stumbled through the dirty streets of Chelsea?

CHAPTER 14

The Harvard Christmas Party

During our months in Massachusetts, Timothy had spent most of his daylight hours in Cambridge, reading, studying, attending Harvard Divinity School lectures, and taking exams. I spent my days in the basement of Chelsea's First Baptist Church day care center working with impoverished preschoolers.

When Timothy handed me the engraved invitation to his Harvard professor's annual Christmas party, I clapped my hands and jumped up and down. "Now I get to see how the other half of Massachusetts lives!" I said. "It'll be nice to be around people with clean faces and manicured fingernails, who know how to use a fork and a knife."

Dressed in my long velvet skirt—after the dry cleaners had removed every trace of Johnny's "sweet potato surprise" handprints from it, I powdered my nose and put on lipstick. I cleaned and polished the tiny diamond of my wedding ring. Timothy had paid Kay Jewelers five dollars a week for many months to buy that engagement ring for me. That evening I felt just like Cinderella—taking a break from the ashes and going to the Ball. The air was crisp and cold that December night, and lightly falling snowflakes added an extra hint of magic to the evening.

The party was held at the Reverend Professor Doctor Armand Smyth's home on the campus of Harvard Divinity School. He lived with his wife in the elegant "Miss Michael's Manse," a mansion built in the late eighteenth century, and once home to the single daughter of one of Harvard's wealthy aristocratic donors. Rumor claimed Miss Michael had lived there to her dying day after her rich handsome suitor left her waiting in her wedding dress at the church altar and never showed up. Legend put Miss Michael in a yellowed wedding dress for the length of her long life. It was said she never removed the wedding cake from the manse's banquet table. It sounded more to me like Miss Havisham in Dickens' *Great Expectations*, but I kept my mouth shut. Anyway, who was I to question a Harvard professor? I did, however, peek into the dining room to see if a wedding cake lay molding on the banquet table.

The Reverend Professor Doctor Armand Smyth himself met us at the door of the estate and welcomed us to Miss Michael's Manse. Beside him stood his beautiful wife, Mrs. Reverend Professor Doctor Armand Smyth.

It's nice to meet you, Reverend Professor Doctor Armand Smyth," I said and slightly bowed toward the master of the house.

"Oh, Denise!" he laughed. "We are friends now that you are in my home! Please free feel to call me Doctor Armand Smyth."

The three-storied house smelled like pine and cinnamon and candied apples. I closed my eyes, put my nose in the air, and breathed in the fresh rich aroma. A nine-foot high Christmas tree, laden with silver and gold ornaments, filled the entry hall. Tiny white lights blinked all around me. Bright red poinsettias in large gold pots sat on every step of the great winding staircase. Florist flowers mixed with red-berried holly leaves sprawled across every white linen dining table. Angels made of fine porcelain and china furled their wings heavenward and beckoned us to eat, drink, and be merry—to celebrate the glorious season of feasts and friends and burning yule logs in wall-sized fireplaces.

Men in black ties, and women dressed in silk gowns and white minks surrounded the banquet table, its surface stacked with the finest imported foods. Shrimp, scallops, crab legs, caviar, and freshly-caught fish delicacies covered one end of the table. A four-foot high ice-carved angelic sculpture hovered over the desserts—large strawberries dipped in rich dark chocolate, almond cream puffs from Switzerland, raspberry tarts, dainty English lemon tea cakes covered with white sugar icing. Under the wings of the gleaming ice angel, every inch of the long banquet table (that supposedly once held Miss Michael's moldy wedding cake) tempted us with every kind of festive food. I had never before seen such offerings all on one table. The tired, old table legs groaned under the bounty it held.

"Hey, Timothy," I said as I picked up my plate and headed through the buffet line. "I like this. Wish my daycare preschoolers could taste this stuff! Would you mind if I asked for a 'doggie bag'?"

"Don't you dare!" he laughed.

After the large group of guests tasted at least one of every imported delicacy on the table, our host motioned for us to retire to the drawing room.

I overheard Mrs. Smyth tell one of the serving maids: "Callie, please dispose of the rest of this food. I think we've all eaten all we care to eat."

"But Mrs. Smyth," Callie protested. "We have so much food left. I can wrap up this food and save it until tomorrow. It'll keep in the refrigerator."

"No, Callie!" stated Mrs. Smyth. "I want it thrown away. Left-overs aren't very tasty the next day."

I looked at Timothy and he looked at me. We were both thinking the same thing: "doggy bag." "Don't you dare ask!" he smiled.

When the guests reached the drawing room, each of us sat down and sank into plush velvet chairs.

Noticing the diamond-studded rings on all ten fingers of the woman that sat beside me, I attempted to initiate a conversation.

"What beautiful rings!" I exclaimed. "Your jewelry is magnificent!"

"Thank you," she said. She held her hands up to the chandelier's crystal light and wiggled her heavy-laden fingers. "I have many more at home. I just need more fingers to wear them all! My husband, Dr. Clyde H. Sombey, VI—he's the CEO of Boston Federal Bank, you know—buys them for me for every special occasion. He tells me that if I ever fell into Boston's Bay with all my diamonds, I'd sink right to the bottom!"

"You must really love jewelry!" I said trying to keep the conversation alive.

"Oh, no honey!" she laughed. "They're just ... Ah ... insurance. I don't know when the good Dr. Clyde H. Sombey, VI, is going to meet Wife #5! And I just want to be ... Ah ... prepared."

She laughed politely, and then looked down at the tiny diamond wedding ring on my left hand.

"Oh," she said. "And your ring is ... is ... it's ... Ah ... *cute!* Yes ... that's the word—*cute!* What a *cute* diamond you have."

I slipped my left hand under my left leg, and sat on it.

Our host began the group conversation by commenting on his recent trip to Rome where he and His Holiness, the Pope, enjoyed an afternoon cup of tea together.

"Yes," said a woman sitting two people away from me, her hair swept up in a fashionable French knot and held in place with a diamond tiara, "the Pope is a lovely man. I had a lovely lunch with him on my last trip to Rome. He, himself, escorted me through the lovely Sistine chapel and showed me the lovely private art collection hidden within the Vatican's vaults. Lovely. Lovely. The public never sees that lovely art collection, you know."

A tall, Clark Gable look-alike who taught Systematic Theology, chimed in. "I'll be lunching with the Pope next week at the Vatican. Shall I tell His Holiness you send your best wishes?"

"Oh, please do," everyone responded in unison.

"Timothy," Mrs. Smyth addressed my husband. "I hear you and Denise live in Chelsea?"

"Yes, we do," he told her. "We chose to live there and work with the congregation of Chelsea's First Baptist Church."

"My goodness!" stated Mrs. Smyth, and placed her right hand on her heart. "I can't imagine anyone actually 'choosing' to live in Chelsea!" She smiled and shook her head from side to side.

A heavily-perspiring woman, wearing a full-length mink coat, laughed. "Honey, I roll up the car windows if I must even drive by that city! I simply cannot tolerate the odor."

More laughter. "I'd be afraid to walk down Chelsea's main street in broad daylight!" another woman piped in. She nibbled the edge of a Swedish pastry. "I would never consider spending one night in Chelsea, much less live there!"

"Surely you two could afford a little flat in Cambridge and move away from those ... those people," suggested Mrs. Smyth.

Before Timothy or I could speak, a tall slender woman who lived inside a model's body, walked into the room and smiled at the Reverend Professor Doctor Armand and Mrs. Smyth. Immediately all the men in the room sprung to their feet and bowed in her direction.

"Ladies and gentlemen," a professor announced. "This is the infamous French writer, Madame Bovaire, author of the best-selling book *The Fabulous Future of France*. She has just flown in from a book-signing in Paris."

"Bonjour," Madame Bovaire said and smiled. Suddenly, without warning or instruction, all the guests began to speak in French, asking the author about her worldwide travels, and complimenting her latest book that everyone-who-was-anyone had read. For the next hour, I had no idea what was said. The only words I knew in French were *soupe du jour*. But I pretended to know. I laughed when everyone laughed; I looked surprised when everyone looked surprised; I ....

I unexpectedly heard my name spoken in English.

"Denise," asked Dr. Smyth. "Timothy tells me you play classical piano. Are you familiar with Beethoven's *Moonlight Sonata*? It's my favorite of all his works."

Feeling like Cinderella before midnight, I smiled and tried to appropriately blush at the compliment.

"Yes, I do." Then I stretched the truth a bit and announced: "I've played Beethoven's Moonlight Sonata on the stage for a large group of people. It's a ... lovely, lovely ... piece of music."

Timothy's eyebrows arched so high, they touched his hairline. Then they burrowed sharply downward, and he looked me directly in the eye and slightly shook his head from side to side. A definite warning.

Never had I felt quite so important. Did they know that a skilled pianist sat in their midst? A pianist that had played before a "large group"? I enjoyed the moment of recognition and admiration, and I fully expected the conversation to return to Madame Bovaire and *The Fabulous Future of France*.

But it didn't.

Mrs. Smyth spoke up: "How wonderful, Denise!" she exclaimed. "Would you honor us, and Miss Michael's concert grand piano, by performing the *Sonata* this evening?"

My stomach turned a flip. I swallowed hard. My body felt frozen. It was as if the clock had struck midnight and

I had turned into a pumpkin. The Reverend Professor Doctor Armand and Mrs. Smyth, and all their guests looked directly at me. Timothy's face fell forward in his hands. I looked at the 12-foot cherry-carved concert grand piano that stretched clear across the room. I put my hand to my chest to see if my heart was still beating.

Me?! I thought. *Play Miss Michael's piano when, no doubt, Beethoven's great-grandson is probably a guest in this very room?!* My eyes still wide and my body frozen in place, I wondered how many real accomplished concert pianists sat sunk into the plushy velvet chairs all around me.

I realized I couldn't say "no". I quickly decided that if I had to play Miss Michael's concert grand, I'd better do it with pretended confidence and throw in some Southern charm.

I looked into the eyes of Mrs. Smyth: "Yes, madame," I said calmly and with pseudo-assurance. "I'd be honored to play Miss Michael's grand."

Timothy peeked with one wide eye between the fingers that covered his face.

Here goes, I thought. I rose from my chair, my chin purposely held high, my velvet skirt flowing around my legs, and I wondered how in the world I'd pull this off. I also wondered in what violent way I was going to kill Timothy for telling the Smyths I played the piano. "Just wait till we get home, Timothy!" I mumbled under my breath as I passed by him.

I slowly walked to Miss Michael's piano and prayed to God I'd remember in what key Beethoven wrote his *Moonlight Sonata*. I had last played the piece at my 10-year-old piano recital, and had used only two of my ten fingers. A large group of ear-plugged parents endured every note. I tried to remember the notes, a decade before, as they were written in my piano book: "Teaching Little Fingers to Play Piano."

I sat down on the bench where Miss Michael herself had, no doubt, many times sat in her worn, yellowed wedding dress, and I raised my hands high in the air. My fingers became unwilling thumbs, uncoordinated, and refusing to work together. But I played the notes, as best as I remembered them, and I played them loud and with drama. My two fingers flew across the ivory keys just the way Mr. Bellhammer and "Teaching Little Fingers to Play Piano" had taught me. When I finished, I noticed that the room was deathly quiet. For a long time. Then I heard a single polite clap. Then another clap. And finally the whole room was clapping in a strained sort of way. I rose from the bench, smoothed my long velvet skirt, and I bowed gracefully toward my guests. Keeping my head high, my eyes focused forward, and a smile plastered on my face, I walked slowly, straight and tall, away from the piano, past the guests in their plushy chairs, past the great banquet table, out the front door, and into the arms of the old green Plymouth Satellite parked between the charcoal-gray Mercedes and the black stretch Limo. Timothy said quick red-faced good-byes and followed me to the car.

"Beethoven would be proud, Denise," Timothy laughed as he cranked up the car. "Exactly what was that you played?"

"You are in big trouble, Timothy," I cried as we drove out of Miss Michael's driveway, away from Harvard, out of Cambridge, and back to the real world. "Big trouble! Just take me home, Timothy! Back home to Chelsea!"

"Okay. I'll take you home," he said. Timothy was no longer laughing.

"And next time," I told him with gritted teeth, "when a certain very *hot place* freezes over, and we go back to Miss Michael's Manse, I'm asking the Reverend Professor Doctor Armand Smyth for a doggy bag! a BIG doggy bag!"

Timothy laughed, and so did I.

"You certainly earned it!" he said.

"And so did all the guests!" I said.

Chapter 15

Home Again

The next morning, I had hot tea and gingerbread cookies with Mrs. Bena and told her all about the party.

"Beethoven must have turned over in his grave," I laughed and described how I had, with two fingers, personally butchered his *Moonlight Sonata*.

"You handled that stressful situation well, Denise," she said. "I wish I had been there to clap for you!"

She smiled with a knowing grin as I described the 4-foot tall sculptured ice angel, the shrimp and scallops, and the English lemon tea cakes sparkling with white sugar icing.

"It sounds delicious, dear," she said. "I'm glad you enjoyed the evening."

"You know, Mrs. Bena, the people there in Miss Michael's Manse were perfect and beautiful, the décor and Christmas decorations exquisite, the food gorgeous and delicious, but I really didn't enjoy the evening. The Smyths were hospitable and kind, but I felt awkward and uncomfortable. And I couldn't stop thinking about how that one ice angel sculpture could have paid twice for Johnny Cornflakes' new shoe."

Mrs. Bena smiled, patted my hand, and reheated my cup of tea.

"I expected that reaction from you, Denise," she said. "You and I have both learned that ice angels melt, and all we have left is a puddle of water to clean up."

That morning, as I laughed and sipped tea with Mrs. Bena, I knew I had rather be sitting with her in that small apartment, located between Chelsea's tire factory and the city's dump, than surrounded by all the food and finery in the banquet-sized dining room of Miss Michael's Harvard-yarded Manse. For the first time since we had moved there, I actually appreciated the city of Chelsea.

The conversation with Mrs. Bena made me more determined than ever to find Johnny Cornflakes. I might not be able to play Beethoven's *Moonlight Sonata* in front of rich, Mayflower-descended aristocrats who drank tea with the Pope, but surely I could find one old man with white wispy hair and an unsightly deformed foot.

CHAPTER 16

Johnny's New Home

As I walked home from Mrs. Bena's, I made a few visits around town inquiring about Johnny. Surely someone in this city would know something about his whereabouts. But I couldn't find anyone who knew anything about him or where he might be. He seemed to have no past, just appearing one day on the dirty streets of Chelsea. Late that night, as Timothy and I lay in bed listening to the planes and sirens of the city, a sudden thought crossed my mind.

"Timothy," I said, sitting up in bed. "Johnny saved my life. He risked his life to save mine. We've got to do something for him. We can't let him freeze to death out on the streets of Chelsea this winter. It wouldn't be the ... uh ... *Christian* thing to do."

"What do you have in mind?" Timothy asked.

"Well, we have that garage room downstairs. I mean we could clean out all the junk and make it into a room for Johnny. At least he could live there during the freezing winter months."

"That's not a bad idea, Denise. The garage is underground so it stays warm. It has a separate door that Johnny could use to go in and out. It even has a window so he could get some sunshine. And we could repair that old toilet and shower that haven't been used for three or four decades. Might work."

With that affirmation, I put my plan into action. The next morning, I woke early and, with coffee in hand, I walked down the basement stairs to inspect the garage room that was to become Johnny's new home.

It would take a lot of work to make it into a decent bedroom, but for some strange reason, I was beginning to care a little something about the old man with the mysterious past. At the very least, I felt sorry for him. I imagined that garage room would soon become a castle to him. He might feel like a king down there in his own quarters.

"It'll be a lot of work," I told Timothy later that morning after I had inspected Johnny's new home. "But Johnny will be delighted. Can't you just see the expression on his face when we tell him about it?"

I spent that afternoon down in the garage room, cleaning, vacuuming, and scrubbing the old toilet and shower (which, with a few adjustments, checked out in workable condition).

Timothy and I, with the help of Jason and Paul, moved the guest room twin bed down the stairs to the garage room. With all the junk cleared out, the room began to take on tones of a real bedroom. "We just need some pictures on the wall and maybe a table and comfortable chair and a lamp," I told Paul. Paul later mentioned the needed items to Mrs. Bena, and she showed up with a borrowed truck filled with wall pictures, a table, a chair, and a lamp taken from her own home. She also brought a plate of cinnamon cookies for Johnny's welcome.

"Let's use these sheets on the bed," I suggested, as I unwrapped the plastic from my new wedding gift sheets.

"I wonder when he last slept on clean sheets?" I said.

From my bedroom closet, I took Aunt Gertrude's quilt. I noted again the tiny handmade stitches and the scraps of cloth she had quilted into colorful designs. It was certainly a gift of love from Aunt Gertrude to me.

Perhaps Johnny will be able to sense some of Aunt Gertrude's love as he sleeps beneath this quilt, I thought.

As Paul, Jason, Timothy, and I stood admiring the beautiful room, Timothy spoke up. "There's just one major problem, Denise. We don't have any idea where Johnny is. How do you suggest we find him to invite him to live in this room?"

I had already considered that problem. "We're going to search throughout all of Chelsea for Johnny," I told him. "And we're going to find him!"

Lisa and Jenny arrived at the parsonage first. Later that afternoon, Rick joined Jason, Paul, and me. While they searched the streets of Chelsea, I stayed home and made dozens of phone calls asking people to help us locate Johnny. Hours passed with no news of Johnny. I continued to telephone church members, hospitals, jails, shelters, and restaurant owners throughout Chelsea asking each one if they had seen Johnny recently.

I knew I was wasting my time, but I decided to call Mrs. Copley anyway.

"Mrs. Copley," I asked. "Have you seen Johnny Cornflakes in the past several days? We're looking for him and have no idea if he's dead, alive, or moved out of town."

"Well," stated Mrs. Copley. "I haven't seen him. Frankly, Denise, we'd all be better off if he's dead or moved out of town."

Mrs. Copley's harsh words brought a sudden ache to my heart. Mrs. Copley had everything a person could want ... And then some. Poor Johnny had nothing—not even a peanut butter and jelly sandwich to call his own.

"I'm sorry I bothered you, Mrs. Copley," I said as kindly as I could. "Thank you for talking with me. Goodbye."

I called Grady's Diner last. "Grady," I asked. "This is De—"

"I know who you are," he barked. He had immediately recognized my Southern drawl before I told him my name.

"Grady, have you seen Johnny?"

"Nope!" he shouted into the phone, as he dragged on his cigarette and called out orders to tired waitresses.

The group searched the streets of Chelsea all day. About ten o'clock that night, Timothy called off the search and the group came home.

They couldn't find Johnny. The temperature had already dropped below freezing. It was too cold to keep searching. They had just walked in the back door when I received a phone call from dear old Mrs. Bena.

"Denise," the familiar voice said. "I have Johnny here in my parlor."

"You're kidding!" was all I could think to say. "Where did you find him? How did you convince him to come inside? Is he okay?"

"Oh, honey," she replied. "You're asking too many questions. When you telephoned to ask for my help, well, I just knew some of the right people to call to find him," she said. "I think I can keep him here long enough for you to drive over and pick him up. But you had better hurry, dear," she added. "He seems awfully restless, and I'm not sure even my sugar cookies can keep him here much longer."

Timothy and Paul hopped in the Plymouth Satellite and drove to Mrs. Bena's to claim Johnny Cornflakes. I made one last telephone call before Johnny came to his new home.

"This is Denise George," I told the elderly woman who answered the phone. I assumed she was Sam's grandmother or his landlady. "May I please speak to Sam?"

"He's at a friend's house tonight," she told me. "But he'll be back in the morning. Can I have him call you?"

"Thank you, but I don't need to talk with him. Would you please just give him a message? It's very important that he receive it. Could you tell him to come to the parsonage tomorrow morning and bring the new shoe we've been keeping for Johnny Cornflakes? He'll know what I'm talking about.

"I'd be glad to. I'll tell him first thing in the morning," she said politely and hung up the phone.

I couldn't wait to see Johnny's reaction when he saw the finished room. And I also couldn't wait until our little group finally presented him with his new custom-made shoe.

When Timothy and Paul helped Johnny into the house, I noticed that the old man clutched a whiskey bottle to his chest.

"Johnny," I said, reaching for the bottle. "We've got a big surprise for you, but let's leave the liquor outside."

Johnny reeked with the stench of alcohol. I wondered if the smell would wash out of the new sheets and Aunt Gertrude's quilt. But it didn't matter. In my mind and heart, Johnny was quickly becoming one of the "least of these" that Jesus described in the gospel of Matthew. And I was going to feed him, clothe him, and provide him with comfortable shelter. In fact, I single-handedly was determined to change his life.

Just wait until the city of Chelsea sees Johnny Cornflakes when I'm finished with him, I thought. *They'll probably name a building after me or give me a plaque.*

Johnny hesitated when I took away his whiskey bottle. At first I didn't think he would let me take it. But I was determined that Johnny would leave his alcohol outside. The church parsonage was certainly no place for a bottle of whiskey. Anyway, when Johnny saw his new room, he'd sober up, straighten out his life, and give up all his bad habits—and his liquor. *Who knows,* I thought, *Johnny might become a respectable Chelsea resident.*

If my arm had been long enough I surely might have patted myself on the back for the miracle I was going to pull off. I felt proud of myself that day—too proud.

We helped Johnny down the stairs to his new room. But he had drunk too much whiskey to notice the clean sheets or the handmade quilt. We took off his worn shoes and tucked him into bed.

"He'll be so surprised when he wakes up in the morning," I said, misty-eyed. "I can hardly wait to see his reaction when the sun comes up and he discovers he has a home. He'll probably never stop thanking me for all I've done for him."

Early the next morning, I scrambled eggs and smeared toast with jelly. *Feed the hungry.* I poured a cup of hot coffee and a tall glass of orange juice and set them on the tray by the plate. *Give drink to the thirsty.* Then I carefully made my way down the basement stairs to the garage room.

"Johnny," I called, and tapped lightly on the door. I imagined that Johnny's poor head would be throbbing, so I had brewed the coffee extra strong for him.

"Johnny," I called again. Balancing the tray on one arm, I turned the doorknob to his room. I knew he was probably still asleep. I wondered if I should wake him for breakfast or just let him sleep.

He'll appreciate a hot breakfast, I thought, and I switched on the lamp. "Johnny?" I called to the bed with crumpled covers.

"Johnny!" I called again.

Johnny hadn't heard me because Johnny wasn't there.

I pulled back the covers to convince myself he wasn't lost somewhere in the new sheets. Putting the tray beside his bed, I looked in the closet, in the bathroom, and under the bed.

But Johnny was gone. I ran through the house trying to find him. As I bounded into the kitchen, trying to figure out what had happened to him, someone knocked at the back door.

"Johnny!" I exclaimed as I opened the door. "How did you lock yourself out of the…."

But it wasn't Johnny. It was Sam who stood outside the door and gave me a puzzled look. "Were you expecting Johnny, Denise?" he asked as he waited for me to invite him into the kitchen.

"I thought you might be Johnny," I sighed.

"But Grandma told me that Johnny was here with you. Look," he said as he held out the large box. "I got your message and I brought Johnny's new shoe."

"Well I've got bad news, Sam," I began. I felt the frustration start to build inside me. "Johnny's gone. He must have left in the middle of the night or early this morning."

I remembered the whiskey bottle I had placed on the back porch. "Just a minute," I told Sam and walked to the corner of the porch and then returned to the kitchen. "And he must have taken his whiskey bottle with him," I said.

CHAPTER 17

The Call from the County Morgue

I didn't have the heart to walk back down the basement stairs to the garage room after Johnny disappeared. Lisa came over that day, made up the bed, turned out the lamp, and brought up the breakfast tray and Aunt Gertrude's quilt. I felt sorry for the old man, but something inside me loathed him for destroying my dreams of making him into a first-class, church-going citizen.

"Once a drunk, always a drunk," I muttered under my breath. Johnny had not even bothered to thank me for all the hard work I put into making the garage room a home for him. He could have at least had the decency to thank me. Maybe Johnny was hopeless after all. Just how could a person help "the least of these" when he didn't want to be helped, when he wouldn't cooperate with all the wonderful plans I had made for him?

Later that morning, I phoned Mrs. Bena and told her the whole story. She remained quiet for a few minutes, and then spoke.

"Denise," she began. "Sometimes we must do for others what God puts on our hearts to do. That's certainly what you did when you provided the room for Johnny. But things don't always work out the way we expect or hope they will. We can't always be assured that the person we're trying to help will accept our love and help. And we can never expect them to appreciate what we try to do for them. We just have to do our best and leave the rest to God."

"Thank you, Mrs. Bena. I know you're right," I told her. "You are such a wise woman, Mrs. Bena. I love and admire you so much. I don't quite know what I would do without you."

"I'm glad our paths crossed, Denise. Surely God put us together here in Chelsea because we both need each other," she said.

That early afternoon, I flipped through my Bible and read the story recorded in Luke 17. I saw how Jesus had been approached by ten men who had leprosy and begged him for healing. Jesus had pity on them, and he healed all ten. But only one man came back and thanked Jesus. The other nine men never came back to say "thanks". The passage of Scripture gave me a new insight into helping others, and confirmed Mrs. Bena's words to me earlier that day.

As I pondered God's Word, the ring of the phone interrupted my thoughts.

"Hello," I answered. "Yes, this is the parsonage. Yes, Timothy George is pastor of the First Baptist Church. He's in the next room. Hold on a moment and I'll get him."

As Timothy picked up the phone and listened to the caller, I noticed his face took on a grave expression.

"Yes, Johnny was here last night," he told the caller. "No, he wasn't here when we woke up this morning. We think he must have left sometime during the night. We don't know why."

Then Timothy's face grew ashen. "Oh, I'm so sorry to hear that. Johnny – frozen to death? The poor man. Yes, I can come down and identify his body."

Identify his body?! The old man I had been hating for the entire morning was dead?! Frozen to death?! Hadn't Timothy just said those words? When Timothy hung up the telephone, I had an explosion of questions to ask him.

"Timothy, is Johnny dead?!

"I'm afraid so, Denise," Timothy whispered, shocked himself at the tragic news.

"Who called you?"

"The county morgue," Timothy answered. "They said they wanted to have one of the city's clergymen identify the body."

Timothy zipped up his heaviest jacket and left the house. I heard the crunch of frozen rain and snow as he stepped down onto the sidewalk.

Why? I asked myself again and again. *Why didn't Johnny stay in his nice warm bed last night? Why did he venture out into the freezing temperature and deep snow when he could have been warm inside our home?*

"The crazy old drunk!" I heard myself shout. I reached for Aunt Gertrude's quilt, wrapped myself deep within its tiny stitches and fluffy stuffing, sat down on the couch, and cried. That's when I remembered why I cared so much for the old man who cared so little about life and who reeked of alcohol. I remembered the night he stood beneath my bedroom window and risked his life to protect me from the gang of youths with their crowbars and their evil intentions. Johnny took a hard blow to the stomach for me. Why wouldn't he let me repay him with a warm bed and a good breakfast?

I knew I had many phone calls to make. For some reason, I dialed Mrs. Copley's phone number first.

"Mrs. Copley? This is Denise George. I'm sorry to have to tell you this, but Johnny Cornflakes froze to death last night. I'll let you know when we'll be having his funeral service. I just thought you'd like to know, since you're part of the church and you knew him."

"Good riddance, I say!" were her first words. "We are all better off with him dead!"

I couldn't believe my ears. I fell silent for a few seconds. Then I heard Mrs. Copley say: "And don't call me about the funeral! I certainly won't be attending the service!" With those words, she slammed down the phone.

Tears filled my eyes and splashed down my face as I dialed Mrs. Bena's number. When I told her the sad news about Johnny, she cried unashamedly into the phone. When she could speak, she said: "Denise, know that you made his last night on this earth a good one. It was the first time he had slept in a real bed in two decades. Even though he didn't personally thank you for your kindness to him, I know he deeply appreciated you...and loved you for ministering to him."

"Thank you, Mrs. Bena."

"Please, dear, let me help you plan the funeral service. Just tell me what I can do to help," she said.

It was a dark day for me, even with Mrs. Bena's encouraging words. I sat down and tried to work up the courage to call the Bible study teens to tell them the sad news. I knew they'd be heart-broken. I yearned for Timothy to return and help me call them.

The wind had picked up since morning. I expected rain or sleet or more snow any moment. I hoped Timothy would come home before the storm started. A tree branch scratched against the living room window. We had one small tree in our fenced yard. I worried that the strong wind would uproot it.

I heard the car pull into the driveway, and I rushed to open the back door for Timothy.

"What are they going to do with Johnny's body?" I asked Timothy as he stepped into the kitchen. "Mrs. Bena said she could help with the funeral preparations. I need for you to talk to the Bible study teens—I don't think I have the heart or courage to tell them that Johnny's dead."

"Wait a minute, Denise!" Timothy said. "One thing at a time. Please ... sit down and let's talk."

I sat down, wiped my eyes, blew my nose, and stared into Timothy's eyes. "I really did love the old man, Timothy," I cried.

"I really did try to help him, and with a somewhat pure heart," I told my husband.

"I know, Denise, but ..."

"I really did appreciate his trying to save my life and ...."

"Wait, Denise! I've got something to tell you," Timothy interrupted. "It wasn't Johnny! The frozen body wasn't Johnny! No one knows who the old man is, but it isn't Johnny!"

It took several seconds for me to digest his words.

"You mean Johnny Cornflakes is still alive somewhere? He hasn't frozen to death?" My mouth flew open and my reddened eyes showed my bewilderment. I felt a surge of happiness that I hadn't felt for a long time. I wanted to jump up and down in excitement like a little girl presented with a new Barbie doll. Johnny was alive after all! I could hardly believe the good news! And I could hardly wait to call Mrs. Bena, ... And Mrs. Copley!

I instinctively glanced at the fireplace mantle and at the large box Sam had brought over earlier that morning—the box that held Johnny's brand new shoe.

CHAPTER 18

The Fire

"Well, wherever Johnny is today," Timothy told me, "I hope he'll find some shelter. The wind is blowing hard, and it looks like we're going to have a whopper of a storm."

The day grew darker and an ominous cloud covered the city as the wind picked up and blew discarded trash across town. I was the first one who heard the fire truck siren scream down the hill from our house. I opened the front door to see what was happening. I immediately smelled smoke.

"I'll bet another apartment building or something is on fire," I told Timothy, who had come to the front door to investigate.

A few minutes later, Jason ran by our house. "The tire factory's on fire," he yelled as he ran down the hill toward the factory. Jason's face was flushed and his hands were knotted into fists. "I'm going down there to see if Mrs. Bena is okay!" he shouted.

"Bring her back to the parsonage, Jason!" I called.

"There'll be a lot of people who won't have homes or jobs tomorrow if that factory burns down," Timothy said.

I prayed a serious prayer for Mrs. Bena's safety, as well as all the daycare's preschoolers' families who lived near the factory. Soon the smell of burning rubber filled the air. It was a strong, stifling smell that was picked up and carried by the unusually swift wind. We soon learned that the fire was quickly spreading into other parts of our city. Chelsea's firefighters couldn't bring the flames under control.

I worried that my family back in Tennessee would hear the news and panic. I picked up the telephone and called my parents. Long-distance calls were expensive and I rarely made them.

"Daddy," I said. "There's a fire in our city, and it seems to be spreading by the wind. Don't worry about us if you see the story on the news. If it spreads much more and comes our way, we'll leave the city. We'll call you and let you know we're okay."

The fire raged all afternoon. The intense wind picked up the flames and carried them from one wooden apartment building to the next. Businesses, restaurants, and public city buildings fell one by one into the grasp of the flames. Oil-burning furnaces exploded time and time again as the flames swallowed up old buildings.

I felt a great relief when Jason finally came to our house with Mrs. Bena. She was shaken up, but otherwise okay. Her house, located next to the tire factory, had burned to the ground. I wrapped her in Aunt Gertrude's quilt and made her lie down on the couch and drink a cup of hot tea.

Exhausted Chelsea firefighters trudged through the snow and worked until midnight trying to control the fire that threatened to ravage the entire city. Other cities had sent their own fire trucks and firefighters to help put out the Chelsea fire. But the fire seemed to have a mind of its own. It leaped at random from building to building, and sent residents scurrying out into the icy streets clutching only their most treasured possessions. They had no time to pack their belongings or dress their children.

The flames were too swift, too sudden. I watched with grief and fear from my bedroom window as the flames shot up into the midnight sky. Fiery fingers of bright yellow, orange, and red reached up above the skyline. Exploding furnaces sounded like rapid gunfire. People crowded the streets, running in insane directions, trying to escape the destruction of the city.

At 1:00 a.m. I asked a practical question. "Do you think we need to pack our things, Timothy? Do you think the fire will reach this part of the city?"

"I doubt it," Timothy responded. "I think the parsonage, church, hospital, Grady's restaurant, Mrs. Copley's house, the grocery store and the pawn shop on this street will be saved. That is, unless the wind does something weird and the fire burns in this direction."

At 2:15 a.m., Mrs. Bena had finally fallen to sleep on the couch. Someone knocked on our front door, and she sat straight up, wide awake. When Timothy opened the door, a soot-smeared face appeared. Out of breath, the frustrated firefighter told us to start packing.

"We're going to evacuate Bellingham Street next," he shouted. "We've already evacuated Shurtleff Street. Better pack what you can carry and get ready to leave."

"What's going on out there?" Timothy asked the firefighter. "What can we do to help?"

"We're just asking the citizens to leave the city as quickly as possible," the fireman said. "We can't get this fire under control. We've already lost three fire trucks to the flames. We'll be battling the flames in front of us, and the wind will whip the flames up behind us. We can't move the fire trucks fast enough to keep them from catching fire."

Again I picked up the telephone and made a long-distance call to my parents.

"Daddy," I began. "We're going to evacuate our house in a little while. The fire has changed directions again and is coming into this part of the city."

"We've been watching the news reports about the fire," Daddy told me. "Are you okay?"

"We're fine, Daddy. But please don't worry about us if you try to call and the telephone lines are down. We'll be okay ... And safe."

"Your mother and I are praying for you, and we have our whole church praying too. Please call us and let us know how ...."

The phone went dead. I heard Timothy's frantic call coming from outside the house.

"Denise! Come help me! Turn on the outside water faucet!" he shouted.

Mrs. Bena and I ran out into the front yard. Sparks of fire and embers were landing on the roof. Timothy had the garden hose in his hands, pointing it at the roof. "Turn on the water!" Timothy called, expecting a blast of cold water. But nothing happened.

"Turn on the water!" Timothy called again.

"I did! I turned it on!" I yelled back.

"The hose is frozen up!" he cried. "With all the sparks, the roof will go up in flames!"

I ran to Timothy. The air was thick with smoke. Apartment buildings had already caught fire on Shurtleff Street. We received another urgent message from a running firefighter. "Evacuate! Evacuate! Leave this area immediately!"

I ran into the house and grabbed Mrs. Bena's coat. What did I want to save? Mrs. Bena followed me. "What do you want to save, Mrs. Bena?! I asked.

She pulled a quarter from the pocket of her faded housedress. "This is all I own now," she said and smiled. "This quarter and my coat!"

With Mrs. Bena in her coat and safely outside, my eyes searched the living room—there was no time to hesitate. Did I want to save the family photos, the new typewriter, the quilt, the silver tea service? I didn't know. I couldn't make up my mind and certainly couldn't carry it all. Again I heard the firefighter order us to evacuate.

"Hurry up, Denise!" Timothy shouted, his arm wrapped securely around Mrs. Bena's shoulders.

For some reason, the large box on the fireplace mantle caught my eye. In a split second, I thought about how much Johnny needed that shoe and how much our little group of teenagers had sacrificed and worked to earn enough money to buy the shoe. In my mind, I could see Mrs. Bena bent over and picking up tin cans in the city dump to add her money to the donation. I surely didn't want to be the one to have to tell them that Johnny's new shoe had burned up in the fire. I made my way quickly to the mantle and grabbed the shoebox. Planting it securely under my arm, I stopped and took one last look back at the silver tea service, my most prized possession. Then with the box under my arm, I made a wild dash for the front door. Within minutes, firefighters took over Bellingham Street, soaking everything in sight with their huge water hoses and fighting the flames that still threatened to consume the whole city.

Timothy, Mrs. Bena, and I, and the other residents of Chelsea trudged through the crowded, smoke-filled streets in a desperate attempt to leave the burning city. We stopped frequently to help mothers carry their children, and to help the elderly on walkers escape the flames.

When we finally stood safely on the outskirts of Chelsea, I stopped and checked for the parcel I had stashed under my arm. To my relief, it was still there. Timothy, Mrs. Bena, and I had somehow escaped the roaring flames with our lives—and with Johnny's $113.92 shoe.

Chapter 19

A City Destroyed

If I live to be a hundred years old, I will never forget the way Chelsea sounded, looked, and smelled when the sun finally came up. Sometime in the early hours of the morning, the winds calmed down and the firefighters finally contained the flames. We walked back into the city, coughing through the thick black smoke that covered everything like a heavy, woolen blanket. The snow on the ground had been partially melted and blackened by soot.

At least half of Chelsea had been completely destroyed. Great hulls of burned fire trucks lined the streets. Firefighters sat exhausted on the curbs, too tired to get up, their faces in their dirty hands. Only the shells of apartments and businesses remained in the part of Chelsea closest to the tire factory. The residents with their children and neighbors stood outside the leveled buildings and cried loudly. No one had expected the fire to do so much damage.

With the exception of crying women and children, a deathly silence covered the city.

"Had the wind not been so swift," one man told us, "the fire wouldn't have been so unpredictable and widespread."

"I heard that some gang members purposely started the fire in the tire factory," another Chelsea resident told us.

"Thank God no one died in that awful fire," Mrs. Bena said. "It looks like plenty of people were hurt, but thank God no one died. That's a miracle!"

"Let's check out the church and parsonage," Timothy said as we made our way through the bevy of broken-hearted people to Shurtleff Street. I braced myself to see the old rock church with its beautiful stained glass windows and tall steeple lying in ruins, and what was left of our house.

When we arrived at Bellingham Street, Lisa, Jenny, Rick, Sam, Jason, and Paul met us there.

"Thank God you are all okay!" I said as I hugged each soot-covered teenager.

"The church and the parsonage are still standing," they told us to our unexpected relief. "There was some damage to the roof, but other than that, they're in good shape."

Sure enough, even through the smoke and cinders that filled the air, the untouched stained glass windows of the church caught a ray of sunshine and sparkled a welcome to us.

"It's a miracle," I exclaimed. "A miracle."

While the flames had devastated one side of the city near the factory and dump, the fire had spared the other part of the city. Not only had the church and parsonage been saved, but the hospital, Copley Manse, Grady's restaurant, the grocery store and pawn shop. Grady was serving up breakfast to the hungry, homeless residents, and grocery store and pawn shop business was thriving too. The hospital overflowed with people who had burns and smoke-filled lungs. The rest of Chelsea's population stood speechless, wondering where they would go and how they would feed their children. Most had lost everything they owned, including decorated Christmas trees and hard-earned Christmas gifts beneath those trees.

It took a full week before the smoke cleared. Since our church proved to be one of the only big buildings still standing in Chelsea, we opened the doors to the people. They came in droves, sleeping on blankets and cots, eating what little food we could find in the church kitchen. So many people came to find shelter, we couldn't house them all.

Timothy decided to call Mrs. Copley and ask for her help.

"Yes?" Mrs. Copley said when she answered her telephone. "Yes, Reverend, I am okay. I was fortunate. My house received no damage whatsoever. And all my valuables are safe and sound, as I am inside my house."

"I'm so glad to hear that, Mrs. Copley!" Timothy told her. "And I have a favor to ask of you."

"What is your request, Reverend?" she asked.

"The church is filled up to capacity with families who have lost their homes, clothes, food, and everything they owned. They have no place to go. Their babies are hungry and crying. We have filled up the church parsonage with cots, but we are going to have to start turning people away because there is simply no room for any more."

"And what do their problems have to do with me?" Mrs. Copley asked.

"You have a huge house, Mrs. Copley," Timothy said. "Could you please allow some of Chelsea's families – who now have no homes and no place to sleep tonight – to move into your house with you? It won't be for long. Help will be coming. But right now we're in an emergency situation."

"I'm sorry," spoke Mrs. Copley. "I can't help you, Reverend. I have the condition of my house to think about and protect. Their dirty clothes and bodies would ruin my antique furniture. And my valuables—those people would steal everything I own. I am locking my doors and staying inside until the smoke clears."

"Thanks anyway, Mrs. Copley," Timothy told her. "I wasn't sure you'd be willing to help. By the way, do you have enough food to eat 'while the smoke clears'?"

"Yes, thank you, Reverend," she answered. "I have plenty of food stored in my cupboards and in my cellar. I am always prepared for emergencies."

Food became scarce while we awaited help from surrounding cities and states.

"What are we to do in the meantime?" I asked Mrs. Bena. "We can't let all these people go hungry?"

Mrs. Bena handed me her coat. "Here, Denise, take this down to the pawn shop and see if you can get a couple of dollars for it." Then she handed me the quarter in the pocket of her housedress. "I wish I had more to give," she said.

I hugged Mrs. Bena and thanked her. Then I walked inside my front door toward my silver tea service. Taking a long last look at the prized wedding gift, I felt a pain in the pit of my stomach. I laid Mrs. Bena's coat down on the sofa, picked up the silver tea service treasure, and headed to the pawn shop.

I left the pawn shop with $36—not much money for so valuable a set. I bought some canned food at the nearby grocery store, and returned to the church kitchen.

Chapter 20

Aftermath

Jenny, Lisa, and Rick took charge of the church kitchen, opening the doors to a team of volunteers who offered to cook and serve food to the community's cold and homeless. Within days, great vats of food began to arrive at the church. Nearby communities and states also sent blankets, clothes, and warm coats for the children. Sam and Paul organized the clothes closet. Donations came in from around the world, even from as far away as Australia. Daily we sorted through pounds and pounds of new and second-hand clothing, dividing the clothes by sizes and helping Chelsea's victims find enough to wear.

The work was exhausting and we seldom had time to sleep. Our group of dedicated Bible study teens worked beside us twenty hours a day to help meet the overwhelming needs of Chelsea's people. Streams of people continued to pass through the church's open doors. They sought shelter, warmth, counseling, financial help, clothes, and food. We had never worked harder or longer. The whole city seemed to fit into the category of "the least of these."

By the week before Christmas, the city had settled down somewhat. Many families had traveled to the homes of relatives or had moved to other parts of the state. Mrs. Bena stayed with us at the parsonage, as well as many other families. Residents ventured out to new areas, new jobs, and new futures. People needed less help from us than before. Our supply of food and clothes had all been given to the needy.

On Friday night, Christmas Eve, our exhausted group of teenagers, Mrs. Bena, Timothy and I met together in the basement of the church to resume our Coffee House Bible study. We sat in the metal folding chairs and listened to the sound of the guitar. After a brief Bible study, we prayed a prayer and bundled up to go home. It didn't seem much like Christmas Eve. We were tired, and too much sadness surrounded us. We missed the people who had moved away from Chelsea. We wondered if Chelsea would ever be rebuilt.

"You know," Sam said. "We've been able to help a lot of people over the last two weeks."

We nodded our heads in agreement. It had been a rewarding experience, but a devastating one, too.

"But," Sam continued, "there's still one person left to help."

We turned to look at one another. Had we left someone out? Was there still a family who needed our help? Who needed clothes or food?

"Who are you talking about?" asked Lisa.

Softly, Sam spoke the name of a person we had not thought about since the fire. We had been so busy, worked such long hours, and offered help to so many of Chelsea's residents that we had forgotten the one person we most wanted to help: Johnny Cornflakes—the very least of "the least of these."

CHAPTER 21

The Search

Before we left the church that Christmas Eve night, I asked a question. "Well, what shall we do? We've got to find Johnny before we can help him. We've not seen him since the fire. We don't even know if he is still living in Chelsea, or even still alive."

Lisa spoke first. "I think we should go out tonight and look for him."

"I second the motion," Mrs. Bena said.

But Jenny disagreed. "I don't know about you guys, but I'm exhausted. The temperatures are dropping and it's already freezing outside. It's much too cold to start searching tonight."

"We could wait till morning and then look for him," Rick spoke up.

"But tomorrow is Christmas Day. And we've planned to spend the day delivering Christmas dinners. We won't have time to search for Johnny," offered Jason.

"I'll go along with whatever the rest of you decide," said Sam. "But I vote for finding Johnny tonight."

"I second the motion," said Mrs. Bena with a twinkle in her eye.

For the next few minutes, we sat still and thought about our options. Jenny was right. It was extremely cold outside, too cold and snowy to be out running around the city. But Christmas Day would be too busy to search for Johnny.

"We could always wait until after the holidays and then look for him," Jason said.

That settled it. We decided to wait until the first of the new year and then resume our search for Johnny Cornflakes.

We put on coats, hats, scarves, and gloves, locked the front door of the church, and each of us headed in a different direction for home.

Timothy unlocked the back door of the parsonage for Mrs. Bena and me, but before we went inside, I stopped him.

"Timothy," I asked. "Do you really want to wait another week or so to give Johnny his new shoe? I mean, wouldn't it be great if we could give him the shoe for Christmas?"

"I second the motion," said Mrs. Bena.

"But Denise," Timothy reminded me, "we agreed to ...."

"I know we agreed to wait," I interrupted. "But do you think you and I could go out and just look a few places where he might be? We could look for about an hour. If we don't find him we can give up and come home."

Mrs. Bena smiled. "I second the motion," she said.

"You love the old man, don't you Denise?" Timothy grinned.

"No, Timothy, it's not that I love Johnny, it's just that ... Ah ... I feel sorry for him. And I don't want the county morgue calling us again to come identify his frozen body!"

"Okay," Timothy agreed. "But don't get your hopes up, Denise. Johnny could be hundreds of miles away from Chelsea by now."

Mrs. Bena leaned over and whispered in my ear: "Get your hopes up, Denise! I believe we can find him!"

"Before we go, let me call Grady," Timothy said. He walked into the kitchen and picked up the phone.

"What do you want?!" Grady shouted into the phone when he answered the call.

"Grady," Timothy asked, "have you seen Johnny hanging around the diner?"

"Don't bother me about Johnny!" he barked. "I've got enough to do right now without worrying about that old man! Business has been booming since the fire! But, to answer your question—NO! I haven't seen him."

Click. The phone went down hard.

"Grady hasn't seen him," Timothy told us. I lifted the large shoebox off the fireplace mantle and pushed it up under my arm. Dirt and smoky soot now covered the once white box. But the shoe inside was intact and clean. Timothy reached for the flashlight.

"Are you sure you're up to this, Mrs. Bena? You probably should stay here inside while we search for Johnny." I said.

"I'm absolutely up to this!" she replied, and grabbed her walking stick.

This time I led the search. I walked as fast as I could so we could cover as much territory as possible before our one-hour time limit ended. Mrs. Bena kept pace. Unlike the last few searches, this time I, too, crawled under apartment porches, checked out some local restaurant alleys, searched the city's trash bins, and walked the dirty, wet street calling his name.

The three of us combed the city for forty-five minutes without a clue about the whereabouts of Johnny Cornflakes.

"Denise, I think this is hopeless," Timothy finally said.

The words choked in my throat. "I guess you're right, Timothy, but let's look just one more place. If we don't find him at Grady's Diner, then we'll go home."

"But, Denise, Grady told me he hadn't seen Johnny," Timothy reminded me.

"But, Timothy, it's our last hope," I said. Even though Grady had told Timothy Johnny wasn't there, I was just stubborn enough to want to check it out myself. "Let's look this one more place."

I looked back and smiled at Mrs. Bena. "I know, Mrs. Bena, you 'second the motion' to keep looking for Johnny!"

"Absolutely!" she said.

Chapter 22

Christmas Dawns in Chelsea

We walked through the snow on Christmas Eve calling Johnny's name as we headed to Grady's Diner. I imagined Grady would be standing by the large dirty grill, where he always stood. He'd probably be serving up some Christmas Eve dinners to hungry folks still left in Chelsea. I didn't care much for Grady, but however rough he was, somewhere buried deep inside Grady's hairy, tattooed chest, I recognized my beloved grandmother's heart. He, too, like her, had a heart of gold that genuinely loved society's down-and-outers, little barefoot girls selling worn dish rags, and old town drunks begging for hand-outs.

Mrs. Bena, Timothy, and I shivered from the cold. Muddy water soaked our gloves and shoes. Sleet began to pelt the desolate city as we walked through dirty piles of snow to the back door of Grady's Diner.

"It'll be a miracle if we find Johnny here," I told Timothy. "But I don't know where else to look for him."

"Miracles often happen," Mrs. Bena told us, "especially on Christmas Eve."

The alley was dark, too dark to see anything. We shined our flashlight around the diner's back door entrance and I prepared myself to be disappointed. *Maybe it's just not meant for us to find Johnny,* I thought.

"Are you okay, Mrs. Bena?" I asked. "You must be freezing and exhausted by now."

"I'm fine, dear. Let's just keep looking for Johnny," she said.

The alley was empty ... except for ... could it be?

"Timothy, shine the flashlight at the corner of the building!" I shouted. And there, caught in the narrow beam of the flashlight was a ... shoe! Yes!

"Look Timothy!" I shouted.

Mrs. Bena jumped up and down—as best she could with her walking stick—and clapped her hands.

A huge dirty old shoe with a large gaping hole was all I saw, but I knew that behind that building's corner lay the old man we had painstakingly searched for. The shoe held a valued prize—a twisted mass of un-socked foot that belonged to the one and only Johnny Cornflakes.

"I'd know that shoe anywhere," I told Timothy. "That's Johnny's foot!"

The three of us ran around the corner and our eyes immediately landed on the figure of Johnny—sprawled out asleep in the alley, soaking wet, and covered with mud.

"Johnny!" I cried. "We found you!"

I couldn't believe we had actually found the old man. I knelt down close to him to see if he was still alive. Yes, he was still breathing.

"Johnny," I pleaded, "tell me you're okay! Are you okay, Johnny?"

Mrs. Bena knelt down, took the old man's hand in hers, and whispered in his ear: "John, John dear, are you okay?"

Johnny looked up at the sound of Mrs. Bena's voice and smiled. "Yes, Margaret, I'm okay. Just very cold, and very tired."

Then Johnny whispered something into Mrs. Bena's ear, and both of them smiled at each other and nodded their heads. "Yes, John," Mrs. Bena whispered back to him, "I remember our walks together. Those were the golden days for us."

I could hardly wait to tell Johnny the good news. "Johnny, we've got a gift—a Christmas gift—for you. It's from the Bible study group at the church."

I knelt closer to the old man who had spent a lifetime sprawled out in one alley or another, while Timothy gently pulled Johnny's worthless foot from his weathered shoe. I opened the box under my arm and unwrapped the new shoe.

"Look, Johnny," I smiled. "Look what the Bible study group bought for you."

The three of us together tenderly placed Johnny's deformed foot into the new shoe. It was a perfect fit. As we tied the long shoestrings, the back door of the diner swung open.

Grady, himself, came out into the alley, looked around the dark corner, and squinted his eyes. In his huge hands, he carried a plastic bag full of food scraps.

"Johnny?" Grady called out loud. "Is that you out there, old man? Where've you been?"

Grady seemed as glad to see Johnny as we were. Surely the heart within Grady beat as happily as our own hearts. Grady flipped a switch on the outside wall and a dim yellow bug light parted the darkness.

"Here's some supper, Johnny," Grady said. "Better get out of the snow, old man. You'll freeze to death." Then he added with a deep rough voice and a rare grin, "And Merry Christmas, Johnny. Merry Christmas to you."

As he tossed the bag of food over to Johnny, Grady hesitated. In the low glow of the yellow bulb, he saw me sitting close beside Johnny. He looked me square in the face and made a statement that made my heart skip a beat—maybe two.

"Here, lady," he said. "There's probably enough for you in there, too!"

As he shut the back door, I caught my yellowed reflection in the glass. I was shocked by what he had said and by what I now saw.

There I was, kneeling in the alley beside the town drunk, my hair wet and disheveled, my clothes covered with mud and snow. I had never been so humiliated in my life. How dare he! Grady had certainly misjudged me. He couldn't see beneath the layers of city dirt to know who I really was. No one had ever spoken to me like that. An appalling thought came to mind: *he thinks I'm a bag lady!*

I looked again at Johnny, who now sat up and stared at his new shoe. Tears slid down his cheeks and dropped off his stubbly chin. Overwhelmed with gratitude, he couldn't speak. Instead, he turned his entire body toward me and gazed at my face with those same bloodshot eyes. Then he opened his food-encrusted, toothless mouth, and smiled. The smell of body odor and old alcohol met my nose, but for some reason I wasn't repelled by it. My hand no longer reached out to cover my face. Instead, it reached out and touched Johnny's face. And feeling an unexpected tenderness for him, I smiled back.

"Forgive me, Johnny," was all I could say as I knelt in the snow beneath the yellow bug-bulb. Feeling the warmth and softness of his face, I added, "Perhaps, Johnny, I have misjudged you, too."

Johnny raised his eyes up to those of Mrs. Bena's. She smiled at him, bent and kissed him on the cheek, and whispered: "I love you, John—I have always loved you ... in spite of you."

Johnny smiled and whispered: "I know, Margaret."

A long silence prevailed before Timothy broke the silence. "Guess what?" he said, looking at his watch. "It's 12:01 a.m. It's Christmas Day!"

"Merry Christmas, Johnny!" I shouted.

"Merry Christmas to you," Johnny answered. "And thank you," he added. "Thank you for caring."

In the predawn hours of Christmas morning, in a dark alley in Chelsea, Massachusetts, Johnny Cornflakes helped me learn a profound lesson about life and love and the simple compassionate act of caring. In God's eyes, we are all precious and valuable, every person, every "least of these"—whether we are a shaggy-haired teenager, a spoiled pastor's wife, or an old town drunk with a brand-new $113.92 shoe.

Chapter 23

The Homecoming

Somehow, in those early hours of Christmas morning, we managed to convince Johnny to come home with us. Timothy slipped off his gloves and put them on Johnny's rough, red hands. When we helped him to his feet, Johnny instinctively picked up the old weathered shoe with the gaping hole in the toe. I guess after so many years it had become a part of him.

The four of us slowly walked home. Mrs. Bena wrapped her arm around Johnny's waist and helped support him as he walked. He put his arm around her bent shoulder. I marveled at how natural the two of them looked as they walked arm in arm. Each time we passed beneath a street light, Johnny stopped, held up his foot, and looked at his new shoe. Perhaps he was trying to convince himself he wasn't dreaming.

Once home, Mrs. Bena scrambled up a dozen eggs and several mugs of hot chocolate.

"I added cream to your eggs, John, just like you like them," Mrs. Bena whispered into Johnny's ear as she served him his plate.

"Thank you Margaret," Johnny said.

Exhausted from the search, Mrs. Bena, Timothy, and I tucked Johnny into his bed in the garage room, covered him with Aunt Gertrude's quilt, and headed upstairs to get some sleep ourselves.

We all slept until the late morning hours of Christmas Day. When we finally woke up, we made quick telephone calls to Lisa, Jenny, Rick, Sam, Jason, and Paul.

"You'll never guess who we found last night at Grady's Diner," I told each of them. "Yes! Johnny Cornflakes! He loves his new shoe. Yes, it was a perfect fit!"

I passed the phone to Timothy. "He's still downstairs asleep," he said. "Yes, you can come over and we'll wake him and surprise him together."

One by one the teenagers gathered in our kitchen. Mrs. Bena scrambled more eggs and fed each hungry person. After we filled the hot chocolate mugs two more times, we decided it was time to wake up Johnny.

"We'd better make this quick," Jason said. "We've got lots of church Christmas dinners to give out today."

Together, excitedly, we tiptoed downstairs and knocked lightly on Johnny's bedroom door. I put my ear to the door, expecting to hear him still loudly snoring.

But I heard nothing.

Timothy quietly opened the door, and I turned on a soft light in his room.

But Johnny was gone.

Unlike before, this time he had neatly folded back the sheets and had smoothed the quilt. On top of the table by his bed, he had left us a "gift" – his old dirty worn out shoe – to him, a precious gift.

"Leaving his old shoe is Johnny's unique way of saying thank you and Merry Christmas to all of you, Denise," Mrs. Bena explained.

"Mrs. Bena," I said, still somewhat puzzled about their 'John-Margaret-cream-in-his-eggs' relationship. "You seem to know a lot about Johnny Cornflakes."

"Yes, dear," she smiled. "I do."

CHAPTER 24

Christmas Evening

For the rest of the day that memorable Christmas Day, our little group carried turkey and dressing dinners to all the families in Chelsea who would otherwise enjoy no Christmas feast. Some women's mission groups from the South had sent money for the food, as well as toys for Chelsea's children. In each home, we told the family about God's love for them. Mrs. Bena led us as we sang a carol or two. Then we hugged each member of the family, and walked to the next home.

That evening, as we all together sat exhausted on the floor of the parsonage and relived the events of the day, the telephone rang. Mrs. Bena answered the phone.

"Oh, I'm so sorry to hear that news, sir," she said. "Thank you for calling us and letting us know."

"What is it, Mrs. Bena?" I asked when I saw her sad expression.

"Someone has died," she said. "It was the county and they called us because they know we knew the person."

"Who?" we all asked in unison.

"I hate to tell you, dears," she said. "I just hate to have to share bad news with people I love."

"It's Johnny, isn't it?" I asked, feeling fresh tears gather in my eyes. "I knew this day would come. How I wish he had agreed to live here with us and be safe. Did he freeze to death? Where did they find his body?"

"Oh no, Denise," Mrs. Bena said. "It wasn't Johnny who died. It was Mrs. Copley. Firemen found her at the bottom of her cellar stairs. They said she went down to get a cake from the cellar—she always had a sweet tooth, you know— and she tripped coming back up the stairs. They said she had broken her neck, and she had the rum fruitcake still in her hands after she died. Such a shame. Poor thing. She's been lying down there dead for weeks. Probably fell shortly after the fire."

"We'll need to plan her funeral," Timothy said. "I'll make arrangements at the church."

Two days later, we cleaned up the church steps, polished the pews, and vacuumed the carpet. We bought fresh flowers from the local florist. On the day of the funeral, a chilling rain fell steadily. Mrs. Copley's grown only son flew in from England to attend the funeral. Not one of us knew Mrs. Copley had a son. The old organ groaned a few hymns at the beginning of the service. The Bible study group, Timothy, Mrs. Bena, and I sat on the front row. On the second row sat only four other people: Mrs. Copley's son, Edward Rutherford Copley V, Mrs. Copley's legal advisor and CPA, and an unknown Boston art collector. Timothy read Scripture found in Luke 16:19-26. Seemed appropriate for the occasion. Those on the second row yawned and looked frequently at their watches during the brief service. Before Timothy said the final "amen," those on the second row had already gathered to discuss Mrs. Copley's estate. Five minutes later, as the Bible study teens reverently carried Mrs. Copley's casket out the front door and helped load it into the waiting hearse, Edward Rutherford Copley V, the legal advisor, CPA, and art collector shook hands and each headed for home and office.

Before he left the church, however, Mr. Copley asked to talk with Timothy.

"My mother left no will," he said. "I guess she never felt that she would ever need one. I have just sold all her possessions— her jewels, clothes, paintings, furs, art collection—everything except the house and furniture – to the Boston art collector who attended her funeral. But the house, Pastor, I want the church to have the house. I must admit that Mother complained constantly about Chelsea's First Baptist Church. She didn't like the music, the people, or the street teens that came to your Friday night Bible Study. I once asked her why she attended the church at all. 'Habit,' she told me. 'And our family owns a pew.' "

"I'm sorry she felt that way," Timothy told the sad middle-aged man. "We tried hard to minister to her."

"I know you did what you could," he said. "My mother wasn't one who easily received another's help ... or love. She has no family left, and never had any friends. And she had more money than she could spend in three lifetimes. My mother was a hopeless woman. That's why I'd like for the church to have the Copley Manse. I don't care what you do with it, and as long as you own it, I'll provide the funds needed to keep it going. I will also pay a care-taker of your choice to live there, as well as for house and yard help, and utilities. I'll furnish whatever you need, Pastor, to use it."

"That's very generous of you, Mr. Copley," Timothy told him.

"You're welcome, Pastor," he said and grew silent for a few moments before he spoke again. "You know, Pastor, I don't like to talk about the dead, but you already know my mother was an extremely selfish woman. She shared nothing with others—not her money, not herself, ... And ... not her love. As much as I tried to do for her, she never expressed any love to me or for me. She constantly criticized and berated me. I think she actually despised me. I never held much hope for a mother-son relationship with her. But that's in the past now. I'll have my lawyer draw up the necessary papers today. The house is yours."

"Thank you Mr. Copley," Timothy said. "Will you be going to the burial?"

"No," he said. "I'd rather not."

"I will make sure that she is properly buried then," Timothy said.

As the two men shook hands, Mrs. Bena walked up to them. She had overheard the conversation that had just taken place. As I was getting ready to leave the church, I heard Mrs. Bena say to Mr. Copley: "Could you please give me a few moments of your time, Mr. Copley?" I slipped quietly into a nearby room. Later Mrs. Bena described to me their conversation.

"Could you please give me a few moments of your time, Mr. Copley?"

"I'd love to, Mrs. Bena ... but ... uh ... I have a plane to catch," Mr. Copley replied.

"What time is your flight?" she asked.

"Well ... it's ... uh ... three o'clock this afternoon," he told her.

"And do you have a ride to the airport?" she asked.

"No, but I plan to catch a cab," he replied.

"You've got plenty of time to talk with me," Mrs. Bena said and smiled. "And after the burial, I'll take you to the airport myself."

"But ... but ...,"

"Mr. Copley, I'll not take 'no' for an answer!" she said as she took his arm and led him to a private corner of the room. In her hands, she carried a Bible and a sack of cookies.

They sat down face to face in metal chairs—the old woman with a heart full of love, and the impatient man with a growl on his face. From an adjoining room, I watched Mrs. Bena open the sack and hand him two cookies—an oatmeal raisin and a chocolate chip cookie.

"While we talk," she told him, "you must taste both cookies and tell me which one is better."

Mr. Copley looked like a sad little boy as he held a cookie in each hand and listened to the old woman.

"You may not have had a mother's love, Mr. Copley," she told him. "But did you know that you have a Father's love?"

"My father died a long time ago," he said. "I hardly remember him at all."

"I'm not talking about your 'earthly' father," she said. "I'm talking about your Heavenly Father."

"Oh," he said. "But Mrs. Bena, I don't believe in a Heavenly Father, or in God."

The old woman smiled and then opened her Bible to John 3:16, and started to read: "For God so loved the world that he gave his one and only Son, that whoever believes in him shall not perish but have eternal life." Then she asked: "Have you ever read that Scripture verse before, Mr. Copley?"

"Uh ... no, I haven't, Mrs. Bena."

"Would you like to know what it means, Mr. Copley?"

"I'd like to Mrs. Bena, if only I had the time," he said. "But ... "

"We'll MAKE the time, son," she said.

Mr. Copley purposely looked at his watch and frowned. But he listened to Mrs. Bena tell him of his Father's love, Jesus' death and resurrection, and the hope it could mean to his own heart and soul. As they talked, he became more interested in what Mrs. Bena was saying. Every few minutes, he'd stop her and ask a question about this Heavenly Father. After an hour or so, Mr. Copley was leaning forward, intent and interested in hearing every word that came from Mrs. Bena's mouth. Mrs. Bena flipped through her Bible and read at least a dozen Scripture verses to him. By the end of their conversation, Mr. Copley looked at Mrs. Bena with such concentration, she described him as resembling a starving dog staring at a piece of meat in his master's hand.

"And what is your decision about Christ?" I heard Mrs. Bena ask him.

Mr. Copley bowed his head, wiped his eyes and nose with a fresh starched handkerchief from his pocket, and asked Mrs. Bena to pray for him. "I want to believe in my Heavenly Father and Jesus," he said. "I want to have eternal hope."

After he gave his life to God, Mrs. Bena stood and hugged Mr. Copley.

"I love you, son, and your Heavenly Father loves you too," she told him through her own tears. Then she smiled at him and asked: "Now which of the two cookies did you most like?" He laughed, held up the chocolate chip cookie, and hugged Mrs. Bena again.

As I sat in the adjoining room and waited for Mrs. Bena and Mr. Copley to finish their conversation, I couldn't help but think about all the jewelry, art, and furs Mrs. Copley owned – all those things she had most loved and cared for – being auctioned off to the highest bidders and scattered into the world asunder like ashes in the wind.

And while Mrs. Bena introduced Mr. Copley to his Heavenly Father, under a gray sky, with sprinkling rain and cold winds blowing through the graveyard, Timothy and the Bible study teens left the church to bury Mrs. Copley. Timothy later told me they cried at her graveside not because they especially liked her or missed her, but because they were touched to the heart by the self-imposed, sad, selfish, and lonely life she had led.

CHAPTER 25

The Copley Manse

Later that afternoon, Mrs. Bena drove Mr. Copley to the airport, then came back and joined us as we all gathered over hot chocolate at the parsonage. She shared the good news of Mr. Copley's conversion, and we prayed a long prayer for him. Then we turned our attention to the Copley Manse.

"Do you have any suggestions about what we should do with Mrs. Copley's house?" Timothy asked.

A long silence followed. Then I had an idea. "We have a lot of people in Chelsea who still have no place to live because of the fire," I said. "And we have even more people, like Johnny Cornflakes, who never had a place to live. I suggest we turn Mrs. Copley's Manse into a home for Chelsea's displaced families and down-and-outers."

"That's a great idea!" the Bible study teens exclaimed in unison. "We could take care of every single 'least of these' in all of Chelsea!"

"We can call it 'Hope House'!" said Jason.

"I second the motion," said Mrs. Bena. She wiped tears from her face. "I think Eddy—I mean 'Mr. Copley' would like that idea a lot!"

"But," said Timothy, "I have one request if we decide to do this. I want you, Mrs. Bena, to be the Copley Manse's caretaker. Mr. Copley has promised to provide funds to keep it going, maintained, and repaired. I believe he will pay you a good salary, Mrs. Bena, for living there and loving all the people God sends into its rooms. We can hire housekeepers and cooks to do the hard work with Mr. Copley's promised funds. For some reason, I believe Mr. Copley will be pleased to see his mother's house – Hope House – used to help others."

"I second the motion!" I said.

"I'd be honored to do that," Mrs. Bena said.

Later that week, Timothy signed all the necessary papers, and Mr. Copley's lawyer handed him the keys to the Copley Manse. When we walked into the house, it smelled like death. Cold, uninviting, but perfectly cleaned and kept. We toured the house, walking from room to room, and marveling at the sheer size of the place.

"How did one woman live here by herself with all this space?" Mrs. Bena asked. "She must have been quite lonely here all alone."

Within the month, the house was aired out and ready for its new occupants. Four families immediately moved into the Manse, filling its halls with the laughter of happy well-fed children. Johnny Cornflakes spent two nights there and then disappeared. Mrs. Bena's little brown bottles of sweet vanilla flavoring lined the kitchen windows, and the smell of sugar cookies soon drifted throughout the Manse's 38 rooms. No longer did Mrs. Bena pick up tin cans in the city dump to afford sugar, flour, and butter. Mr. Copley, himself, paid Mrs. Bena a salary for keeping the house, and bought her as much vanilla flavoring and cookie supplies as she needed. Once every six months or so, Mr. Copley's limo arrived at the front door of Hope House, and he sat down at Mrs. Bena's kitchen table and sampled an ample portion of her homemade cookies.

"Margaret!" he exclaimed each time he visited her. "You smell just like vanilla!" He also telephoned her each week from England, checked on her health, inquired about the Manse's residents, and checked on the state of her supplies.

"Margaret," he once said. "I hear that you've been giving away all the caretaker job money I pay you. If that's true, I'd like to request you spend some of it on yourself."

"Thank you, son," she responded. "But I need nothing. And those around me need much."

For the next three Christmases, Mr. Copley visited the Manse, placed a huge Christmas tree in the entry hall, and invited Chelsea's children to decorate it. He also made sure every child in Chelsea had a gift to open on Christmas Day, a children's Bible, a box of Mrs. Bena's gingerbread boys and girls, and an envelope with some much-needed cash. Mr. Copley had not only found his heavenly Father's love, but in Mrs. Bena he had also found a mother's love. And he responded to both loving hearts fully.

Before the fourth Christmas came, we regrettably sent word to Mr. Copley that Mrs. Bena had passed away. He cried for a long time into the telephone when he heard the sad news.

"How did she die?" he asked softly when his tears stopped flowing and he could again talk.

"Her tender heart just stopped beating," Timothy told him.

"She had a big heart full of love," Mr. Copley said. "I'll be there within 24 hours," he said. "I'd like to pay for and help with her funeral."

On the day of the funeral, Chelsea's narrow streets, designed a century ago for horse-drawn carriages, couldn't begin to accommodate the large number of cars that drove into the city from all 50 states and several foreign countries. For the first time in ten decades, every pew in Chelsea's First Baptist Church was filled. And Mrs. Bena's grandfather's skillful fingerprints still graced every wooden pew. When the pews overflowed, people stood around the walls and in the streets to honor Mrs. Bena. I kept turning around and searching the sanctuary for Johnny Cornflakes, but he didn't attend. In fact, no one had seen Johnny for several years.

Timothy preached that afternoon from Acts 9:36, and compared Mrs. Margaret Bena to Scripture's Tabitha "who was always doing good and helping the poor." Timothy asked Sam to read Jesus' words in Matthew 25.

Sam picked up his Bible, turned quickly and easily to the Gospel of Matthew, and read: "For I was hungry and you gave me something to eat, I was thirsty and you gave me something to drink, I was a stranger and you invited me in, I needed clothes and you clothed me, I was sick and you looked after me, I was in prison and you came to visit me."

Sam stopped reading, and wiped his eyes with his sleeve. Then he continued:

"Lord, when did we see you hungry and feed you, or thirsty and give you something to drink? When did we see you a stranger and invite you in, or needing clothes and clothe you? When did we see you sick or in prison and go to visit you?"

"I tell you the truth," Sam read, "whatever you did for one of the least of these brothers of mine, you did for me."

At the end of the service, before the final prayer, Mr. Copley stood up unexpectedly.

"I know this is unplanned," he said, "but may I say something before we close the service?"

"Of course, Mr. Copley," Timothy smiled and said.

Mr. Copley opened his Bible and read aloud: "For God so loved the world that he gave his one and only Son, that whoever believes in him shall not perish but have eternal life." He closed his Bible, but before he sat down, he looked out over the vast number of people in the old Gothic sanctuary.

"Mrs. Margaret Bena introduced me to my loving Heavenly Father," he said. "And over the past several years, I've not only known a Father's deep love, but a mother's love, too."

Then he added: "If you, too, need to meet your Heavenly Father – who loves you with a perfect love – I'd like to personally introduce you to Him after the service."

Thirty-two people of all ages met with Mr. Copley after the funeral. He told them about his life, his transformation, and his appreciation of Mrs. Bena for leading him to Christ. Then he prayed with each person individually.

All 32 people left that day with tears in their eyes and transformed hearts. After everyone was gone, Mr. Copley shook Timothy's hand.

"Thank you, Pastor," he said. "And I'd like you to know I've made two decisions. I will be selling my house in England and moving into the Copley Manse—I mean the "Hope House," as its new caretaker. I want to finish the good work Mrs. Bena started there. And I'll be establishing a trust fund in Margaret Bena's name that will enable every child in Chelsea to go to college and graduate with a degree. I know it's what Margaret would want me to do."

CHAPTER 26

Graduation

Before long, Timothy's graduation day came. We packed what few belongings we had left, walked out the back door of the parsonage, and said some tearful goodbyes to the Bible study teens, Mr. Copley, and our Chelsea friends. I had so wanted to say goodbye to Johnny Cornflakes, but he was nowhere to be found. We were heading South again, to a bluegrass Kentucky town where Timothy would teach Church History. We left in the same old green Plymouth Satellite that we had driven into Chelsea many years before.

But before we left, I ran back into the parsonage. In my hands, I held the quilt, so lovingly stitched by Aunt Gertrude. I decided to leave the quilt in the garage room that day. I thought maybe, just maybe, the new pastor and his wife might let Johnny come back to live there again ... if he ever wanted to.

CHAPTER 27

Chelsea Revisited

It was a decade later before Timothy and I could return to visit Chelsea. We arrived early on a cold snowy Sunday morning. The large stained glass windows still reflected the rising sun and sparkled a familiar welcome to us.

We noticed that Chelsea had been rebuilt since the fire. New apartment buildings mingled with the old buildings still scorched by fire and smoke. We wondered if we would see anyone we had known during our "Chelsea years." As we sat in the still, quiet sanctuary of the huge old church, we silently reflected on the years of hard work and hard prayer we had invested into the lives of Chelsea's people. We wondered if our hard work had mattered at all. Were the Bible study youth still involved in the church? We thought about Mrs. Bena and her kindness and her cookies. We thought about Johnny Cornflakes and wondered if he was still alive.

After thirty minutes or so of quiet reflection, people began to fill the old sanctuary. Young couples holding hands, families with children of all ages, old folks walking on canes, and teenagers coming in groups turned the wintry silence of the empty sanctuary into a blooming, active springtime.

Folks hugged, smiled, greeted each other, and complimented new lacy dresses worn by little girls. The church had definitely grown, its spirit sweet with Christian fellowship. But all the faces around us were new ones. Timothy's eyes met mine and we both thought the same thought. Our Bible study teens could be scattered all over the world by now.

The century-old organ groaned some familiar hymn, the pastor made a few announcements, and everyone quieted down so the worship service could begin. Just then, I felt a light tap on my shoulder. I turned around to see Lisa, Jenny, Rick, Sam, Jason, and Paul beaming on the pews behind us! We created quite a commotion during the next few minutes. Sitting with the now grown "teenagers" were spouses and small children and at least one newborn baby. In fact, all together they filled up two long pews! Even a few former Crypts had joined the church.

I was startled right down to my toes by the next sight I saw. An old man limped up to the pulpit and bowed his head. I didn't recognize him at first. His hair was cut and combed. His fingernails were clean and trimmed. While not the very latest style, his dark suit was neat and pressed. And his shoes – my eyes instinctively lowered to his feet – his shoes were black, polished, and shiny. And they matched!

As I listened to the heartfelt, humble prayer spill from the old man's lips, it suddenly dawned on me. This man, this well-mannered old man – so cleaned and polished – was the one and only Johnny Cornflakes! In bewilderment, I turned and glanced at Lisa, who sat directly behind me. She looked straight at me, a smile formed on her lips, and she nodded her head as if to say, "Yes, Denise, it's Johnny! Can you hardly believe it?!"

Needless to say, after the worship service ended, a great time of reunion followed. All the Bible study "teens" had stayed in Chelsea, had gone to college with the help of Mr.

Copley, had married and raised up families, and had continued to work together to build up the church and community. They had also helped Mr. Copley carry on the work of the Hope House. Mr. Copley had built two more wings to the old Manse, and it could now house more than 20 of Chelsea's needy families. The members of the Friday night Coffee House Bible study group were now Chelsea's leading citizens and the ones teaching the Bible study for Chelsea's new teenaged batch of the "least of these." Under their influence and guidance, Johnny Cornflakes had finally laid down his liquor bottle forever, and had joined the grand old church built the century before from hand-cut rock by Mrs. Bena's grandfather.

"I'm so proud of you Johnny!" I told the old man who stood before me. "That was a beautiful prayer you prayed this morning."

"Do you think Margaret would be proud of me?" Johnny asked.

I nodded my head.

"Yes, Johnny, I do. *Very* proud."

"Thank you, Denise, for all you tried to do for me."

"No, Johnny," I said. "I should thank *you* for all you *did* do for me."

I reached out my arms and, for what was to be the last time on this earth, I hugged Johnny Cornflakes goodbye. And as I turned and left the sanctuary, I smelled the sweet lingering scent of vanilla.

Also available from this author

Our Dear Child
Letters to Your Baby on the Way
DENISE GEORGE

'I'm pregnant!' As soon as you know that your baby is on the way people take notice. Normally relatives soften, total strangers start conversations and family members take extra care of you as you look forward to the day of your child's birth.

Of course there can also be difficulties and complications, morning sickness and sibling jealousy but all in all, preparing for the birth of a baby is a special time.

But what's it going to be like with a baby in the house? How will I prepare for his or her arrival and what will be the best way to nurture and enjoy this time?

Take heart from these encouraging letters written by writers Denise and Timothy George to their yet to be born child. They are honest, heart-warming and full of wisdom.

These short meditations make an ideal gift to anyone contemplating bringing a child into this world and who wants to give them the best start in life.

ISBN 978-1-84550-141-9

God's Gentle Whisper
Developing a Responsive Heart to God
DENISE GEORGE

"Why don't I hear God's voice?" is a thought, maybe even a cry that every Christian has uttered to themselves. We yearn to hear God's voice speak to us but also have a curious impatience for his answers. We live in a society that has only three standards of results – 'I want it now', 'I might just be able to wait until tomorrow' and 'I'll get it somewhere else!' It's not surprising that we can't wait for, or often hear, God's voice in our lives. Denise, a successful journalist, author and public speaker, challenges us to seek an intimate dynamic relationship with God through three aspects of waiting on him in prayer:

* We know him by listening with our heart.
* We love him by hearing his voice.
* We serve him by responding to his gentle whisper.

ISBN 978-1-84550-236-2

Teach Your Children to Pray
Denise George

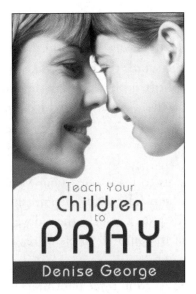

In a nut-shell this book is a non judgmental, practical, hands-on, I've been there approach to Christian parenting ... with a wonderful, inspiring, get me started focus on prayer. Yet it doesn't compromise on the truth and the challenge of God's word. Once you start reading it you will realise the value of prayer, you will be itching to start it with your child, you will learn and your family will learn the importance of communicating with God.

Denise George, is a mother, Christian and human being. Her book is written on the back of a life time of experience, mistakes, triumphs, problems, ideas, inspiration, questions, scripture reading... and prayer.

Every family should read this. Every family should use this. Because every family should teach their children to pray!

ISBN 978-1-85792-941-6

Christian Focus Publications

publishes books for all ages

Our mission statement –

STAYING FAITHFUL

In dependence upon God we seek to impact the world through literature faithful to His infallible word, the Bible. Our aim is to ensure that the Lord Jesus Christ is presented as the only hope to obtain forgiveness of sin, live a useful life and look forward to heaven with Him.

REACHING OUT

Christ's last command requires us to reach out to our world with His gospel. We seek to help fulfil that by publishing books that point people towards Jesus and help them develop a Christ-like maturity. We aim to equip all levels of readers for life, work, ministry and mission.

Books in our adult range are published in three imprints:

Christian Focus contains popular works including biographies, commentaries, basic doctrine and Christian living. Our children's books are also published in this imprint.

Mentor focuses on books written at a level suitable for Bible College and seminary students, pastors, and other serious readers. The imprint includes commentaries, doctrinal studies, examination of current issues and church history.

Christian Heritage contains classic writings from the past.

Christian Focus Publications Ltd,
Geanies House, Fearn, Ross-shire,
IV20 1TW, Scotland, United Kingdom.
info@christianfocus.com
www.christianfocus.com